Social Determinants *of* Moral Ideas

Maria Ossowska

∴

SOCIAL
DETERMINANTS
OF
MORAL
IDEAS

∵

Routledge and Kegan Paul

LONDON

First published in Great Britain 1971
by Routledge & Kegan Paul Ltd
Broadway House, 68-74 Carter Lane
London, EC4V 5EL

Copyright © 1970 by the Trustees of the University of Pennsylvania

Printed in Great Britain
by Unwin Brothers Limited,
The Gresham Press, Old Woking,
Surrey, England
A member of the Staples Printing Group

ISBN 0 7100 7013 6

Contents

Introductory Note

Maria Ossowska is professor of moral philosophy at the University of Warsaw and one of the leading figures in the Warsaw philosophical school. Polish philosophers are best known in the West for their work in logic, but the movement which began with Kazimierz Twardowski at the beginning of this century was equally concerned with clarity, rigor, and method in other branches of philosophy. During her nearly fifty years as teacher in the University of Warsaw, Professor Ossowska has been the principal worker in the field of ethics and a major influence on many students. The task she set herself was to show that moral philosophy can be studied in a scholarly and scientific manner, that obscurities and vagueness can be avoided in this field, and that a moral philosopher does not have to be a preacher. No one contributed more than Mrs. Ossowska to establishing in Warsaw the spirit of anti-irra-tionalism which has proved so valuable in preserving independence of thought during difficult and dangerous times.

Mrs. Ossowska received her doctorate in Warsaw in 1921 with a dissertation on Stoic axiology or value theory. Her thesis supervisor was Jan Łukasiewicz, the logician, classical scholar, and historian of philosophy. It was while collaborating on this dissertation that Łukasiewicz first realized the originality and importance of Stoic logic. Mrs. Ossowska continued work in two of the major fields treated by the Stoics: se mantics and ethics. In Poland in the 1920's the philosophy of language had not yet come under the influence of logic; it was dominated by a psychological theory of meaning as formulated by de Saussure. Mrs. Ossowska analyzed critically various concepts of meaning to be found in the literature of the time, wrote papers on the concept of an expression, the relation between logic and grammar, between words and thought, between *significatio per se* and *significatio per aliud* in Anselm. Her work, together with that of Kotarbiński and Ajdukiewicz, helped to establish the scientific attitude toward semantics that proved to be so fruitful in the later development of the subject.

It was from about 1932 that ethical studies became Mrs. Ossowska's dominant preoccupation. At that time she formulated a program for the study of moral facts, a program which she has been systematically carrying out ever since, together with a number of her students. She divides the study of moral facts into three main groups of problems: 1) meta-ethics, or the analysis of the language used to formulate moral judgment and express moral sentiment: the language of norms and of evaluations; 2) moral psychology, a study of the motives that lead people to take moral stands, including an examination of general theories such as altruism, egoism, and hedonism, construed as explanations of moral behavior, and 3) the sociology of morality, including the description of ideal types of behavior for men in various societies, as exemplified by the model of the knight or warrior-hero, the bourgeois ideal, the explorer or the saint as types. In each of the first two areas she has published one major book; in the third area, the sociology of morality, on which she has been working intensively since the early 1950's, she has produced five books, including the present volume.

Mrs. Ossowska's work in meta-ethics is summed up in *The Foundations of the Science of Morality*, written from 1932 to 1939; the war delayed its publication until 1947. Now in its fourth edition, it is a standard text for philosophy students in Poland. Had it been published when first complete, or had it been translated into English, it would probably have exerted some influence on contemporary British and American work in meta-ethics. The affinity between Mrs. Ossowska and British philosophy is not surprising. G. E. Moore's *Principia Ethica* was one of the first philosophical books she encountered (in her father's library), and she wrote several early articles on Bertrand Russell, including (in 1922) a review of *The Analysis of Mind*. From 1933 to 1935 she had a research fellowship to England, where she became personally acquainted with Moore, as well as with Bronisław Malinowski. During the war she composed her second book: *Human Motivation: An Enquiry into the Psychology of Moral Life*. Her first volume in the sociology of morals was *Bourgeois Morality*, published in 1956; and her work in this area continues with *An Outline of the Sociology of Morals* (1963: originally delivered as lectures at Barnard College in New York in 1960), *British Moralists of the Eighteenth Century* (1966), and the present work which surveys general theories and systematic problems in the social and historical conditioning of moral ideas. It is scarcely necessary for us to summarize the content of this book. We would simply like to point out a certain affinity not only with the work of Malinowski but also with the School of Durkheim with which Mrs. Ossowska was in direct contact during her year in Paris in the early 1920's.

Her book on the British moralists is concerned not only with the principal philosophers from Locke to Bentham but also with legislative changes during the eighteenth century, with the content of novels by Fielding and Richardson, of drawings by Hogarth and Rowlandson, considered as manifestations of moral positions which are related to the theories of the philosophers. The book analyzes critically the view of Weber and the Marxists which attributes the tolerance and religious freedom of the eighteenth century to the economic interests of the middle class who wanted to do business with everybody. By contrast Mrs. Ossowska stresses the fact that people in Great Britain were generally tired of religious war and the pressures of orthodoxy, and that tolerance was thus in part a Restoration reaction against the dogmatic tensions of Cromwell's time. As in the present book, the author assigns an unusual role to Mandeville, whose socio-technological point of view is recognized as an important moment in the history of ethics—an importance largely neglected by historians of ethics, even of utilitarian ethics. In 1970 she published *Moral Norms: An Attempt at Systematization.*

In the long list of Mrs. Ossowska's publications (nearly a hundred papers, almost as many reviews, two translations, in addition to the six books just mentioned), there are two significant gaps: from 1939 to 1945 and from 1952 to 1955. During the former period all universities were closed in Poland and no books were published. A handful of professors organized a clandestine university, meeting with small groups of eight to twelve students in private apartments and teaching a variety of subjects from chemistry to philosophy. (On the one occasion when a class was discovered by the Gestapo, the participants were shot.) Mrs. Ossowska was one of the organizers of this underground university and an indefatigable teacher during the war years. Her ability to conduct clear conceptual analyses in an atmosphere surrounded by police action and military hostilities became legendary. Her late husband Stanisław Ossowski was both a philosopher and a sociologist, and an author who exerted a decisive influence on the political and intellectual life of the war and post-war generations. Together the two of them helped students continue their studies during the war; the Ossowski apartment became a classroom, a meeting place for seminars and political debate, a library where the family books were made available to students. (For some time it also served as a hiding place for a Jewish child.) For those of us who grew up in complete isolation from the outside world, when the University Library was closed and occupied by a detachment of police, these meetings at the Ossowski apartment were a major formative factor in our development as students and as men.

During the second dark period for Polish intellectual life (1952 to 1955), neither Mrs. Ossowska nor her husband was allowed to teach or publish. They were isolated from their students and from public life. In these worst years of the Stalinist period, their independence of thought could not be tolerated. Of this time Mrs. Ossowska has said: "Both in research and in writing, for me these years were like living in a backwater."

Today, though officially emerita she is still giving her seminar in the University of Warsaw, and she is at present writing a book on the concept of the knight as a model of life. As an illustration of Mrs. Ossowska's treatment of moral facts and as an introduction to the present work, we may recall the contents of a paper on physics and ethics which she read before a conference in Geneva in 1958, attended by many leading physicists.[1] She compared the present terror created by the atomic bomb to earlier moments in history when there were widespread forecasts of imminent catastrophe. Europe faced such a crisis in the year one thousand. Famine, plague, eclipse, the eruption of a volcano, together with the very number of the year, were interpreted as portents of the end of the world. But there are decisive sociological differences between the two crises. Today it is not superstition but science, not the ignorant but the experts that warn us of catastrophe. The terrors of the past were confined to a few provinces; those of today threaten whole continents. Finally, in the year one thousand the destruction of the world was seen as the last battle in the war against Satan, and it was God who would be victorious in the end. Both were forces outside man. Today we fear a world annihilation that could be unleashed by man himself. In the last few centuries the triumphant bour-

[1] See *Man and Atom*, vol. XIII of the International Meetings at Geneva, 1958.

geoisie took an optimistic view of the future. An all-embracing belief in progress was almost universal. Today (she said in 1958) youth adopts the attitude of Epicurus: "Live privately" —"the wise man does not take part in public affairs unless circumstances oblige him." For Epicurus this attitude was a response to the feeling of powerlessness on the part of a Greek citizen in the age of Hellenistic empires. The feeling of power- lessness plays an important part in the attitude of modern youth—though, we may add, the response of the young has shifted significantly in the last ten years. In 1958 it seemed to Mrs. Ossowska that the man who has begun to feel powerless must either withdraw from the world or cling to the illusion of power. In formulating the first alternative, she anticipated by a few years the ethos of the hippies, the modern Epicureans who "opt out" in favor of the private life. Mrs. Ossowska recognized the second response in the life of unmotivated violence as practiced by Polish hooligans, English teddy-boys, French zazous. Since then we have seen a new and world-wide public commitment of young people in the politics of con- frontation with a variety of Establishments. Perhaps what is essentially new here must be traced precisely to the fact noted by Mrs. Ossowska in 1958: that in this case the cause of terror and powerlessness seems to be man-made. Hence it is also natural for the young to hope that human effort can control the crisis of our world civilization and prevent the worst.

It was a rare experience to have Mrs. Ossowska as our guest in 1967, when she delivered the lectures which are here published in a revised version. We hope that the present volume—as the first of her major writings to be published in a language other than Polish—may help to introduce the English reader to her work, and to that of a philosophical school that remains largely unknown in the West.

HENRY HIŻ

CHARLES H. KAHN

University of Pennsylvania

Preface

This book is composed of lectures delivered in the Department of Philosophy of the University of Pennsylvania during the Spring semester of 1967. It is divided into four parts. In the first I try to distinguish between different trends of thought in books on ethics, and to point out that some problems included up to now in normative ethics are gaining independence. I also distinguish three main groups of problems to be included in descriptive ethics. These distinctions allow me to place my own problems among others.

In the second, and central, chapter, moral phenomena are considered as dependent variables. Here I aim at a systematization of a number of factors which can be said to influence morality in a given society.

The third chapter is devoted to a discussion of some theories concerning not particular moral phenomena, but morality as a whole.

The fourth chapter endeavors to outline, on the basis of historical documents, two class-determined types of morality, the "nobility" ethos and the "bourgeois" ethos. The book ends with reflections on the concept of morality. What is left of morality after the elimination of problems which more and more live a life of their own still does not form a homogeneous whole, making the definition of morality difficult and threatening the adequacy of theories which treat morality as a consistent body. Fortunately, a sociology of morality can work, as I try to show, to a large extent without a definition of its subject—a situation which is not peculiar to it alone, but which is common to many branches of learning.

Most of my considerations have been published in Polish, sometimes in a much more extensive form. I have, for example, devoted a whole book to the so-called "bourgeois" morality in Polish. A small part of the contents of that book has been translated into either French or English and published in scientific journals scarcely available today. Isolated from my colleagues abroad by the barrier of language, I welcomed the invitation to come to Philadelphia as an opportunity for valuable personal contacts. I am aware how much I owe to Henry Hiż in the publication of this book; without his help it would never have appeared.

M. O.

Social Determinants *of*
Moral Ideas

CHAPTER I

Introductory Distinctions

I shall start with introductory remarks concerning two terms which will be used repeatedly in my considerations. They are *moral* (or *morality*) and *ethics*.

Let us begin with the ambiguous term *moral*.

1. *Moral* is sometimes opposed to *physical*. When someone is hurt in an accident his pain is physical; when he is humiliated his pain is called moral.

2. Sometimes *moral* is opposed to *immoral*, and then it is used as a laudatory term and, like all such terms, is emotionally loaded.

3. *Moral* sometimes refers simply to sexual behavior. This use of the word typically occurs in countries with Christian tradition.

4. *Moral* may mean "tending to improve." We use the term in this sense when we speak of the moral teaching of a fable or of an event.

5. *Moral* may be a neutral term denoting a particular kind of value judgment or precept. We speak of moral valuations as opposed to aesthetic valuations, of moral precepts as opposed to rules concerning the efficacy of our actions, of moral sense as an ability to distinguish between right and wrong and of moral insanity as the disability to make this distinction. *Moral* here refers to a class of phenomena: moral sense, just as is a sense of humor, is a disposition.

Of the five uses of the word *moral* just enumerated, two are commonly confused. When Adam Smith derived moral actions from an innate fellow-feeling in men, he meant by moral actions,

actions deserving praise. For Smith, the fact that we have an innate tendency to react with a smile to someone's smile and with sorrow to someone's distress explains the existence of all amiable and all respectable virtues. They are all based on natural sympathy. "And hence it is—that to feel much for others and little for ourselves, that to restrain our selfish and to indulge our benevolent affections, constitute the perfection of human nature." [1]

Other writers have used the word *moral* in a purely neutral sense. Brand Blanshard contends that "any question is a moral question whose decision depends on a choice between values." [2] For Blanshard the choice is moral, whether the choice be right or wrong.

In our considerations we shall use the word *moral* in this last, neutral sense of *belonging to morality*. Although the word *moral* is the Latin translation of the Greek *ethikos*, these two words became differentiated in many languages. The word *ethics* often means a branch of learning, while morality is supposed to constitute its object. Thus we speak of the morality of hooligans and of the ethics of Aristotle or Spinoza. Ethics is supposed to be found in books, while morality is to be found in life. As the opinions of philosophers concerning right and wrong also belong to "life," being the opinions of their milieu and their time, ethics should be subordinated to morality.

Moral values are thought by many writers to belong to a higher level than other values because they need other values in order to exist. We are blamed for being the cause of unnecessary suffering because suffering is an evil. We are wrong in trying to belittle and humiliate our neighbor because everyone attributes great importance to his own personal worth. The fact that moral values are linked in such a way with other values makes it impossible to study them in isolation. If they are studied against the background of other values, one can refer to the word *ethos* with its wider connotation. According to Robert Redfield, "the ethos of a people is its organized conceptions of the Ought." [3] Other writers use the term *ethos* to denote the general orientation of the given culture, its predominating interests and values, which permit it to be characterized as militaristic or Apollonian, for example. Sometimes, as Redfield points out, "the phrase 'style of life' has come into this discussion to meet the need for a term that will suggest what is most fundamental and enduring about the ways of a group persisting in history." [4] As can easily be seen from these quotations, ethos can be ascribed only to a group. An individual may have a morality, but he cannot have an ethos.

These preliminary verbal conventions are provisional and give no satisfactory account of the difficulties connected with our conceptual apparatus. I shall more than once return to this subject, and more particularly to the very controversial concept of morality. In order to make it clearer, let us turn to books which announce in their titles that they are concerned with ethics. Assuming that morality is the subject of ethics, let us see what kind of problems have been discussed under this heading.

Problems of Normative Ethics

An attentive reader of books on ethics will not fail to be struck by the diversity of problems which they examine. The content of a treatise on this subject can never be known in advance. Not infrequently one chapter might be replaced by some other without any detriment to the composition of the whole, since the choice of questions discussed in the book does not seem justified in any clearly definable way. All this goes back to a very old tradition. In fact, it was the ancients who included under the heading of ethics diverse considerations, to which other subjects were added as European philosophy developed. That incoherent whole represents the venerable heritage of a succession of generations, a heritage which now seems to be breaking into its component parts. Let us examine one by one the principal groups of problems which, in varying proportions, are the subject of treatises on ethics. Thus we shall be able to discover what problems are closely linked with ethics, and whether it is regrettable that certain others have started to live their own lives outside the domain in which they were born.

To begin with, let us divide everything that the ancients called *ethics* into two principal groups of problems, normative ethics and descriptive ethics. Normative ethics covers formulations of value judgments and rules of conduct, while descriptive ethics describes and explains phenomena. Whatever close contacts may exist between these two fields, it is still justifiable to treat them separately. In this chapter, we shall restrict ourselves to problems belonging to normative ethics, that is, ethics in the strict sense of the word. This means that we shall confine ourselves to a discipline—it is safer not to call it science, since its scientific character is disputed—whose purpose is not only to study our conduct, but to guide it.

1. If we analyze treatises on morals, such as the *Nichomachean Ethics* of Aristotle or Aesop's fables, we find there, parallel to rules of moral conduct, rules which have in view not the moral goodness of our behavior, but its efficacy. Aesop tells of a dying man who summoned his sons to his bed in order to persuade them that they should live in harmony after his death. To convince them, he showed them rods which could easily be broken one by one, but when tied in a bundle defied all attempts to break them. This fable extols solidarity, not as a moral value in itself, but as a value guaranteeing the efficacy of our actions with respect to the goal which we want to attain: "united we stand, divided we fall."

Today, problems of this kind are discussed separately, outside the field of ethics, and their autonomy seems favorable to their study. Some authors suggest calling the study of such problems *praxiology*.[5] Praxiology would systematize precepts intended to ensure success of action, that success being sometimes in accord and sometimes in conflict with the moral value of action—which in such considerations does not come in question. In the case of Aesop's fable, cited above, solidarity, recommended by the moralist, is an important factor in success, but the moralist is far from approving some other praxiological rules, such as the principle of *divide et impera*, which by its efficacy has rendered so many services in politics, or the rule of making one's opponent face a *fait accompli*.

2. In the same treatises on ethics we must distinguish considerations which tend to attribute to things their true value, to classify those values that are recognized, and to arrange them hierarchically. These problems form a general theory of value or a general *axiology*. Moral values constitute here only one group among others. It is here that it is appropriate to locate various

proposals to define the notion of value and of related concepts, such as that of interest. Here too we must ask the question, whether all values are reducible to one, namely that of pleasure—an opinion supported by many hedonists. If there are many values, not reducible to one, they must be classified. Traditionally, values have been classified as good, true, or beautiful. Sometimes more differentiating classifications of values are given, for instance according to the interests which they satisfy (Ralph Barton Perry), the needs which they express (Bronisław Malinowski), or the institutions by which they are realized and protected (Stuart Carter Dodd).[6] It is well known to what an extent these questions absorb, for example, the German philosopher, Nicholas Hartmann, in his book on ethics, and what place they occupy in the reflections of the German phenomenologist, Max Scheler who, among other things, strives to establish a hierarchy of values. The problems given here as examples have started to live their own lives. There is a growing number of treatises on values which do not raise any moral questions or do so only incidentally. At present, issues of general axiology often change hands, passing from philosophers to sociologists or cultural anthropologists. The change is usually for the better. Authors who have a sense of the concrete have brought the values placed by Hartmann in a Platonian stratosphere back to the earth and have demonstrated their close contact with man's needs and aspirations. In the process, however, these problems usually cease to be normative in character and form a psychology or a sociology of values. For example, the problems discussed by Stephen C. Pepper in *The Sources of Values* (1958) belong to the psychology of evaluation. Pepper analyzes the attitudes adopted by men with respect to objects appreciated in a positive manner (appetitions) and those attitudes which are manifested in aversions, repulsions, and the like. One of the important questions concerning values in general is whether it is possible to measure value. Whenever we choose we measure. Any preference implies measurement. We measure when we decide the punishment appropriate for a crime or when we distribute prizes for the best execution of a Mozart concerto. Durkheim tried to measure social cohesion by the number of suicides; Robert C. Angell measured the integration of cities by the crime index and the welfare index.[7] So far as we know from recent works concerning the measurement of values, it is possible to build a scale where A would be less valuable than B, and B than C, but it may not be possible to say *how much* less valuable A is than B, or B than C.[8]

3. Treatises on ethics usually reserve a prominent place for instructions on how to attain happiness and, above all, how to avoid suffering or how to overcome it when it is inevitable. It was not without reason that ancient authors resorted to medical terminology. One readily thinks of the *tetrapharmacon* of Epicurus who addressed the unhappy as one addresses the ill. One will also bear in mind similar comparisons used so freely by Seneca and Cicero. The latter considered suffering to be a malady of the soul (*morbus animi*) which should be treated at all costs. The principal preoccupation of the ancient Stoics was to guard themselves against suffering, and it was this preoccupation which accounted for their view that any object of which we can be deprived is thereby valueless.

These problems, which in varying proportions can be found in the works of ancient and modern authors, combine to make a whole that might be called hygiene of inner life, or *felicitology*, a term coined, if I am not mistaken, by Otto Neurath, who was an active member of the former Vienna Circle. This term may shock the linguists with its Greek ending added to a Latin stem, but since an analogous combination has been approved in the term *sociology*, it can also be admitted in this case.

If the starting point be a certain definite idea of happiness, the question may be posed, what are the most efficacious methods of attaining that happiness? The answer to this question must be based on observation. Thus, for instance, we may ask ourselves whether it is reasonable to anticipate all possible disasters. It is true that such anticipation permits us to prepare ourselves for an imminent shock, but, on the other hand, certain disasters which threaten us do not occur after all, whereas anticipation of them is never a pleasant experience. Thus it is difficult to decide whether anticipation of disaster does or does not contribute to our happiness. Further, we may ask whether it is true that one disaster tempers us against a possible new disaster, whereas an easy life makes us vulnerable to any difficulties we may encounter. The view that we do not seek happiness but find it in what we seek and the belief that we have more chances to be happy when we do not think of it, belong to felicitology. It is also the task of felicitology to choose between the two contradictory formulas for happiness. One advises us to have rich and various needs; the other states that to be happy we must live so that our needs are simple and easy to satisfy. All these problems are quite independent of those belonging to the moral order and are best treated separately.

The remedy suggested by ancient sages was aimed at the symptoms and not at the causes of illness. They did not tell us how to organize a society which would not use exile as a punishment; rather they told us what to do, in the event of being an exile, in order to suffer least. When we want to treat the cause of human suffering we now turn either to social reformers or to psychotherapy. Books on mental health which deal with the causes of alienation, maladjustment, stress, or frustration have inherited a large part of the problems discussed previously in books on ethics. But since certain sufferings are inevitable, regardless of the social system in which we live or regardless of our physical condition— for example, the suffering caused by bereavement and by the anticipation of our own death—the precepts of the sages retain their therapeutic value and deserve not to be forgotten.

4. In the reflections of the ancient sages on ethics we discover a fourth group of problems. The authors who tell us what to do to suffer least also tell us what to do to suffer bravely and to die with dignity. The point here is not our happiness but our perfection. With perfection in view we strive to master a fit of anger, and the desire to improve ourselves makes us resort to ascetic practices, whether we are professional ascetics or ambitious adolescents. In order to discover the path to perfection ancient philosophers wanted to know what human nature is like. They thought that the cultivation of those traits that are specifically human would help man to attain truly human dignity. And since it is reason which distinguishes us from other living beings, they claimed that man in his conduct should be guided by reason.

He who aims at personal excellence does not take suffering into account. A social reformer who opens the eyes of the pariahs of the world to the injustice they suffer, merely adds to their misery, but he does so in order to help them live a life worthy of human beings, a life which will conform to a given ideal of personality.

Every man and every group of people has ego-ideals which shape his or its existence. Crane Brinton proposes to call the human ideal type in a given culture "enviable"—an admirable human figure, which can be embodied in a real, living person, or in a fictitious character.[9] The invincible warrior emerging from the epic poems of Homer, the sage, the *civis Romanus*, the gallant knight, fearless and blameless, the honest man of the seventeenth century, the honest bourgeois, the modern gentleman, the American self-made man—all these are examples of models which during entire epochs induced people to self-improvement and imprinted specific traits upon the cultures which had adopted them. Plutarch's *Lives* have been read over and over again for centuries and, according to the well known tradition, Charlotte Corday had a volume of Plutarch under her arm when she went to assassinate Marat. Contemporary cultural anthropologists find themselves unable to understand the culture they study if they fail to discover in it the ideals of personality accepted by the group. Often these ideals are not perceived as such and have to be reconstructed indirectly. In a complex society there are usually several of them, not necessarily adjusted to each other. A person who belongs to several social groups in one society changes his patterns of conduct as he changes his dress, according to the milieu he is actually in. Admired persons induce imitation. But it also happens that it is disdained persons who exert a decisive influence on men and thus guide their efforts: for instance, at the end of the nineteenth century the ideals of the petty bourgeois were an obsession with the Bohemians and by contrast incited them to an opposite, eccentric behavior.

The ideals of a society are tacitly assumed and taken for granted. Only rarely does a philosopher describe his ideal person as Aristotle did when he drew the portrait of the magnanimous man. To find the ideal of human behavior prevailing in a given milieu and epoch we must turn to literature, to educators, to social reformers. It is to Benjamin Franklin, above all, that we owe the ideal of the honest bourgeois in the eighteenth century, and it was Daniel Defoe, the author of *Robinson Crusoe*, who endeavored to adapt the model of a gentleman to the needs of the middle class. Sometimes we can extract ideals from the pious lies which turn a dead person into an edifying figure for the living. Biographies of great personages have often undergone many emendations in order to be exemplary. Irregularities in sexual life have been concealed, political and religious opinions have been adjusted to conform to accepted standards. Several years ago it was discovered that the sister of the French poet Rimbaud had introduced a number of petty corrections into her collection of her brother's letters. For example, when the poet wrote about his budget and his expenses, she would add zeros to figures she believed too modest. Such alterations make very interesting material for the study of ideal personalities.

Efforts to improve oneself in reference to an ego-ideal are generally connected with the need to feel superior to others, and moral superiority has often been associated with social superiority. The term "noble" denotes both superiority of class and of moral behavior. The same applies to the term "gentleman" which denoted a man of gentle birth, but was used by Locke with reference not only to the nobility but also to the privileged classes in general. During the nineteenth century the term came to mean first of all moral excellence, as can be seen from the definitions of the word "gentleman" in successive editions of *The Encyclopaedia Britannica*. "Villain," the opposite of "noble," reveals the same duality by denoting simultaneously social and moral inferiority. Cases of similar duality can be observed in many languages. The ambition to distinguish ourselves by our excellence makes us develop virtues which Eugène Dupréel in his *Traité de morale* [10] describes as virtues of honor. These virtues are difficult to attain, since to distinguish ourselves we must struggle; easy achievements are within the reach of all. In the work of perfecting ourselves aesthetic considerations play no small role and combine with moral evaluations, for the ideals toward which we strive are usually judged with the eye of an artist as well as with the eye of a moralist.

5. Our own happiness and our own perfection were the domi-

nant problems of ethical thought in antiquity. Modern ethical thought, while not jettisoning these preoccupations, prefers to concentrate on questions of social order. In his *De cive* Thomas Hobbes did not ask what to do in order to avoid pain, nor how to live as an ideal human being. He tried to discover how to organize human society so as to avoid conflicts, and what measures should be used to ensure a peaceful life for all citizens.

Certainly these questions were not unknown to the ancients, but, as in the case of Aristotle, they were relegated to the domain of politics. In modern times they are the focus of moral considerations. The development of industry in the second half of the nineteenth century suggested the idea of a society functioning like a well oiled machine. The task of moral rules was to help bring about such a state of affairs. This conception of the role of ethics explains why many authors assert that morality does not exist outside society. This conception brings the ethical writer close to the legislator and turns ethics into a sort of socio-technics, a hygiene of social life. Moritz Schlick was one of several authors who were of the opinion that ancient philosophers were interested solely in the development of personality (*Selbsterfüllung*) and knew nothing about morality in the proper sense of the word. For Schlick, morality was born only when man began to be interested in the restrictions he had to impose upon himself, restrictions necessary to let others live (*Selbstbeschränkung*).[11] This opinion seems to be confirmed by the fact that the opposition between egoism and altruism and the endeavor to harmonize the two have become the focal problems of modern ethical thought.

"We live in society;" wrote Voltaire in the article on virtue in his *Philosophical Dictionary*,[12] "there is therefore nothing truly good for us but that which does good to society. An hermit will be sober, pious, and dressed in sackcloth: very well; he will be holy; but I will not call him virtuous until he shall have done some act of virtue by which men may have profited." Beginning with the eighteenth century, the important, if not the principal, task of ethics becomes that of reducing human conflict to a minimum. The work of Jeremy Bentham can serve as an example of a moral system born of close collaboration between the moralist and the legislator. Social reformers who claimed that in an ideal society, organized in conformity with their recommendations, no morality would be necessary, obviously must have understood by morality, rules intended to make society a harmonious whole. Rules would in fact be superfluous if the organization of life in the community made conflicts impossible. But a good organization of social life does not render superfluous a morality conceived as a set of rules suggesting various ideals of self-improvement.

After the elimination of problems concerning the efficacy of our action, which we have at the outset separated from ethics and entrusted to specialists in other fields, ethics appeared to be confined to four groups of problems: the first was axiology or a general theory of value; the second we called felicitology; the third was concerned with personal excellence; and the fourth was formed by the totality of rules which make human relations harmonious. Normative moral thought is certainly too complicated for all its shades to be preserved in the four groups distinguished above, but this classification explains certain misunderstandings revealed in discussions on moral problems, and makes us realize why certain theories, which claimed to embrace the whole of morality, have proved inadequate.

Since the time of Adam Smith, many ethical writers have wanted to base morality on an innate faculty in man which they call sympathy. The fact that a child responds with a smile to his mother's smile and weeps when he hears others weep accounted for the hope that, by appealing to that tendency which Smith called "fellow-feeling," it would be possible to teach people to have the good of others in view and to make social life harmonious. Smith and his followers were interested in the organization of social life and disregarded problems of personal excellence. Others have wanted to base morality on honor and dignity and were concerned with the perfection of man. Those who attribute an important role to human effort have revealed that they are interested above all in human perfection, while those who take into consideration only the consequences of actions have laid stress on the organization of social life.

Many authors have criticized values derived from one of these theories by applying to them standards borrowed from the other. In his *Principles of Morals*, Hume criticized the privations which ascetics imposed upon themselves. He pointed out to those who fasted and resorted to other severe self-deprivation, that what they did was perfectly useless and could only have a detrimental effect on their character. In fact, such practices would seem more pernicious than laudable to those who organized social life. But such ascetics did not lack either sense of merit in the eyes of those who believed that they could thereby secure eternal happiness or that they were striving toward an ideal personality.

In conformity with the perfectionist theory, we sometimes choose the most difficult path when we seek the good of others. But it is not necessarily true that the greatest sacrifice provides the greatest benefit for our fellow men.

In our moral precepts and also in our theoretical considerations, we constantly pass from one system of ideas to another. The educator who wants his pupils to abhor lies sometimes attains his goal by appealing to their dignity and their sense of shame—a practice recommended by Locke in *Some Thoughts Concerning Education* and intended to play on perfectionist ambitions. He who shows us that lying is dangerous has our happiness in view. This is the lesson of the well known story of the shepherd who cried "Wolf!" just to fool others and who was not helped when attacked by wolves. Finally, there is the moralist who condemns lying because an atmosphere of confidence and mutual trust is necessary for community life. The same three types of arguments are presented by those who recommend that we control our passions. Some people advise us to do so because self-control will protect us from suffering; others because it is indispensable to our moral excellence; still others because it is a necessary condition of harmonious social life.

While it is important to realize to which system of ideas particular statements belong, and while it may seem advantageous to treat these spheres separately, it is impossible not to notice the links which unite them.

Let us begin with the theory of value. Different authors hold different opinions as to the hierarchies of values. If someone recommends to us the most durable values, he evidently has our happiness in view and wants to eliminate the suffering which would result from the loss of such values. If someone else assigns to sensual pleasures a very inferior place in the scale of values, he does so because he holds the opinion, common in Christian thought, that human perfection cannot be linked with values that are shared by both men and animals. And finally, if someone asks us to hold in great esteem those values which lose nothing by being shared—the value of music or of a book is not lessened by being enjoyed by many—he asks us to do so because such values do not arouse conflicts, as is the case, for instance, with values called economic. He who has a good dinner is perhaps depriving one of his fellow men; he who covers himself with a quilt perhaps exposes his neighbor to cold. If one, without realizing it, adopts at the same time different principles for building a hierarchy of values, then one finds it difficult to obtain results that could satisfy the requirements of logic.

Ancient ethics, which, as we have seen, was concerned principally with human happiness and human perfection, combined the two with the conviction that virtue was not only a necessary but also a sufficient condition of human happiness. According to Seneca, happiness followed virtue as the shadow follows the body. That conviction was born of man's need for justice: the human sense of justice revolts against the possibility of evil persons being happy. The desire to see that fate corresponds to merit is one of the most powerful in man. According to Max Weber, this desire contributed to the birth of religions: the gods undertook to ensure just compensation in the other world whenever justice was not implemented in this world. Thus there is nothing astonishing in the fact that, although the concept of virtue has been modified in the course of centuries, the conviction that there is a strict relationship between virtue and happiness persists in spite of all evidence to the contrary. That conviction is found, for example, in the *Fragen der Ethik* by Moritz Schlick. The desire to serve others and to share their pleasures—which, according to Schlick, is an essential element of virtue—gives one most satisfaction, and the fact that goodness and joy manifest themselves in the same facial expression is no pure coincidence. According to him, the pleasure we take in the pleasure of others knows no limits. Not only do we never tire of it, but it increases our own ability to feel happy (*Glücksfähigkeit*). Schlick seems to ignore the fact that a person who is sensitive to the happiness of others and shares it in a sincere manner must in all probability be also sensitive to their sufferings, and that consequently the same inclination accounts for that person's additional happiness and for his additional suffering.

Attempts to determine to what extent our happiness is due to our social instincts date back at least to the time of Charles Darwin. Quite recently, Pitirim Sorokin tried to prove, by means of empirical methods, that, on the average, altruists enjoy better health than do egoists and that consequently, thanks to their attitude of benevolence toward other people, altruists live not only more happily but also longer than egoists.

Those who see human perfection in the disposition to serve others and at the same time believe that such service is an inexhaustible source of happiness, combine the three trends of thought mentioned above (stressing happiness, perfection, and social harmony) by making both human perfection and human happiness depend on civic virtues. But one can easily find systems of ethics in which human perfection has nothing to do with man's virtues as a member of society. An ascetic who, in order to seek perfection in solitude, has broken all his social bonds, abandoned his family, and left for the desert, follows a model of perfection where rules concerned with social life cannot be applied. Certain authors have tried to demonstrate that in the end all virtues, even strictly personal ones, are always advantageous from the point of view of society, but they have never succeeded in convincing us. In a given society, ideals of personality are most often born in a spontaneous fashion, not guided by rational thought, and they often comply with very old traditions of a magical nature. Elements of this kind are to be found in different systems of sexual morality all over the globe. In such cases personal perfection follows its own course, without regard for what would be best for society. In one of his essays Hume suggested monogamy or polygamy according to the relative number of men and women in a given social group. But our system of morality, probably under the influence of Christianity, has turned monogamy into a requirement of personal perfection that does not take heed of the total happiness of society.

Reconciliation between perfection and personal happiness as the basis of morality has never been complete. People who believed they had reached it were confused. It was not happiness conceived as a minimum of suffering and a maximum of pleasure that could be linked inseparably with moral excellence; it was only happiness conceived as true happiness, the latter being inseparable from perfection just by definition as the notion of true happiness always involves an ideal of personality.

We have declared ourselves in favor of an autonomous treatment of the general theory of efficacious action, a theory which was previously studied within the domain of what the ancients called 'ethics'; and we believed it reasonable to study separately the problems of a general theory of value and the problems of felicitology (which resorts to a purely psychological concept of happiness). It remains thus for normative ethics to organize the functioning of society with respect to a given ideal of interhuman relations and with respect to the ideal of personality adopted for the members of that society. In the eyes of modern moralists, these two groups of problems appear inseparable and seem to represent morality in the strict sense of the word. When speaking of morality we shall have them in mind. As Bertrand Russell wrote, "without civic morality communities perish, without personal morality their survival has no value." [13]

Problems of Descriptive Ethics

In the first part of this chapter I tried to distinguish different groups of problems in ethical considerations. But the same books which taught us how to be happy, how to attain perfection, or how to organize society into a harmonious whole also contained an extensive knowledge of facts connected with moral life.

"Moral facts," wrote Durkheim in the introduction to his book on the division of labor, "are facts like any others: they consist of rules of action which can be recognized by some distinctive characteristics; thus it must be possible to observe them, to describe and classify them and to find out rules which explain them." [14]

To combine in the same branch of learning value judgments and norms with purely empirical considerations seems unfavorable either for the elaboration of rules or for the development of our knowledge of moral life. Much confusion is due to this symbiosis. Descriptive ethics ought to be treated separately from normative ethics. Only after they are separated can we realize the tasks descriptive ethics must perform; only then can we see its achievements as well as the problems which have been hitherto neglected and deserve our attention.

I think it is possible to divide problems belonging to descriptive ethics into three main categories, each with its own subdivisions.

1. I propose to put into the first group all problems comprising a meta-ethics. We move in the domain of meta-ethics when we analyze the structure of ethical systems, when we ask ourselves in what sense of the word 'system' these systems can be so treated. We are in the domain of meta-ethics when we discuss the logical character of value judgments and rules, when we dispute the applicability to them of the notion of truth and falsehood, when we analyze the kind of arguments which can be brought in their favor and the kind of persuasion we use to convince our opponents in the absence of such arguments. *Ethics and Language* by C. L. Stevenson discusses those problems. It is an example of a book devoted entirely to meta-ethics.[15]

The problems cited above are far from exhausting the field of meta-ethical considerations. To meta-ethics belongs also the question of what characteristics distinguish moral value judgments and moral rules from aesthetic judgments or traffic regulations.

> . . . We all understand roughly what is meant by morality. . . . We all make the distinction between a man's moral character on the one hand, and his agreeableness or intellectual endowments, on the other. We feel that to accuse a man of immoral conduct is quite a different thing from accusing him merely of bad taste or bad manners or from accusing him merely of stupidity or ignorance.[16]

This rough knowledge of which G. E. Moore is speaking may be sufficient in our everyday practice. When we investigate moral life we must certainly delineate more precisely our field of research, the more so because it is often difficult to decide in a given case whether we are dealing with moral approval and disapproval or not. We all agree that a condemnation of cruelty is a moral judgment, and we agree that a commendation of clear thinking is not. We hesitate to say, however, where the opinion that happiness constitutes the highest value is to be placed. Is it an opinion belonging to morality or does it rather belong to a general axiology elaborating a hierarchy of values?

David Hume, in the first section of his *Enquiry Concerning the Principles of Morals*, in order to discover what he calls the true origin of morals or what constitutes personal merit, undertakes to consider "every attribute of the mind, which renders a man an object either of esteem and affection, or of hatred and contempt; every habit or sentiment or faculty which, if ascribed to any person, implies either praise or blame, and may enter into panegyric or satire of his character and manners." This method leads one to discover "the circumstances on both sides, which are common to these qualities; to observe that particular in which the estimable qualities agree on the one hand, and the blamable on the other." These considerations aiming at the determination of moral facts were treated as the central topic of the descriptive ethic called by Durkheim *physique des moeurs*. Although they are purely empirical, they belong to the group of meta-ethical problems, as they serve to determine the subject of ethics.

The analysis of the structure of ethical systems, of value judgments and norms does not exhaust the domain of the meta-ethical. We must include the clarification of ethical thought in general by making ethical concepts clear. He who speaks about the language used in ethics speaks about ethics too and thus enters the meta-ethical field.

At present, the number of publications treating the problems mentioned above is particularly great. Each year many books and articles are published discussing the nature of value judgments as compared with descriptive judgments, the verifiability of the first, the possibility of applying measurement in the field of moral values, and so on.

2. Another important branch of descriptive ethics consists of all the psychological problems related to moral life.

a) We shall begin by pointing out some interesting problems concerning the process of evaluation. In recent times we have had the opportunity to observe in several countries the tendency

c

to see things as completely black or completely white. This tendency has proved useful in propaganda because the soil was fertile. By this I mean that people in general feel a need to see things as either black or white and to avoid any ambivalence. *Gone with the Wind* by Margaret Mitchell has been translated into Polish and widely read in my country. But I know readers who feel uneasy about Scarlett because she appeals to their hearts in some ways but does not enlist their sympathy in others. The tendency toward uniformity in our attitudes leads not only to seeing things as either black or white, but also to seeking laudable causes for events which we judge to be good and bad causes for events we judge to be evil. This tendency was manifested in the teaching of the ancient Stoics who, against all evidence, thought that right and wrong form two different causal chains which never meet. Bernard Mandeville shocked many of his readers by trying to prove the contrary. In Remark G of *The Fable of the Bees* he wrote, "The short sighted vulgar in the chain of causes seldom can see further than one link; but those who can enlarge their view, and will give themselves the leisure of gazing on the prospect of concatenated events, may, in a hundred places, see Good spring up and pullulate from Evil, as naturally as Chickens do from eggs." In our attitude toward values we recognize a tendency to dogmatism. Our belief in our superiority is strongly supported by a conviction that our hierarchy of values, our way of life, our culture is best.

We have chosen these examples from numerous ones which could illustrate problems of a psychology of evaluation. An investigation of these problems is all the more topical when we realize only now to what extent our attitude toward the world is primarily evaluative. The world seems to us either friendly or hostile and we discover more and more hidden value judgments in all branches of our learning. Value judgments are to be found in apparently neutral economic considerations. Gordon Allport and others showed recently how value judgments dovetail with notions of normality.

b) Problems connected with human motives and intentions belong to a second subdivision of psychological problems. Ethical writers of all time have been interested in discovering whether we are always guided in our activities by expectation of pleasure or by avoidance of pain, whether we always have our own interest in view or whether we are, sometimes at least, guided by a disinterested sympathy. These problems have only rarely been treated in an empirical way, although this is the only way to solve them. They have interested the moralist and the educator because both have wanted to know what they can expect of man and both have wanted to take human nature into account before making their rules.

c) We include in a third section of the psychology of moral life, problems concerning feelings like the so-called sense of duty, remorse, moral scruple, guilt, repentance, moral indignation, and so on.

The theoreticians who spoke of moral sentiments were using this expression in two different ways. Sometimes they meant emotions like those connected with moral approval and disapproval—pangs of conscience, shame, and the like.[17] At other times they were discussing sympathy, love, hate, or aggressive attitudes, having in mind not specifically moral experiences, but emotions or attitudes approved or disapproved by the moralist. The study of the latter belongs to moral education, which accepts a readymade hierarchy of moral values and tries to develop and foster approved feelings and behavior while discouraging or eliminating what is disapproved.

d) Exaggerated forms of these experiences are the object of a psychopathology of moral life. Psychoanalytical writers have shown that the feeling of guilt plays an important role in human life, often in the form of an obsession. Exaggerated and persistent scruples have often been the object of clinical observations and the theme of interesting novels. The question of what constitutes moral insanity belongs also to this section. Last but not least, the investigator of moral life will find many interesting suggestions in the numerous analyses of the antisocial behavior of some dissident groups, which at the present time are of grave concern to educators everywhere.

e) Another class of problems is to be distinguished in connection with the development of morality in the individual, that is, with the ontogenesis of our moral judgments and attitudes. These problems form the central topic of the well known book of

Jean Piaget, *Le jugement moral chez l'enfant* (*Moral Judgment of the Child*). Piaget tries to show the difference between morality developed under the pressure of adults and morality observed within groups of playmates linked by symmetrical relations. Ever since Freud stressed the importance of early childhood for the development of moral attitudes, much has been written on the influence of family life in the molding of our moral personality.

3. The last major section of descriptive ethics is formed by the sociology of moral life. As I intend to treat its problems in a more detailed way later, I shall limit myself at present to a few examples.

First of all, let us review factors which can determine moral attitudes, not of individuals, but of societies as a whole. The subsequent chapters will be devoted to these problems. As we shall see, the determinant role of a factor can be ascertained only in comparative research, a task which is far from easy, as it involves an extensive knowledge of different cultures.

Among psychological problems in the list given above were included the possibility of studying the ontogenesis of morality and of tracing its development in the life of an individual. In the list of sociological problems we shall find a corresponding study of the philogenesis of moral rules and of their evolution in societies. As everybody knows, these problems have attracted attention, particularly since the time of Darwin. According to Darwin, there is a constant progress of morality. Antisocial people are automatically eliminated in the course of evolution, making room for the socially minded and for the altruists, who are better adapted to social life and thus the fittest.

The distinction between problems belonging to meta-ethics and those belonging to a psychology or to a sociology of moral life take into account only systematic problems of descriptive ethics. Till now we left aside all possible historical research in this field which as such has always had a descriptive character. The history of morality is particularly important for those who, denying the possibility of applying the notion of truth in the domain of value judgments and norms, deny also the existence of progress in matters of morals. (This conclusion I do not consider necessarily valid). Whoever denies moral progress or thinks it dubious, should stress particularly the importance of a history of morality, for then a historical knowledge of moral life is something more than a history of blunders overcome, such as is the history of chemistry. It resembles rather the history of art. As the history of art gives us a panorama of different styles, so the history of morality gives us a panorama of different ways of life from which we may choose: the way of life proposed by the Stoics or that proposed by the Epicureans, to name but two.

There are branches of learning whose unity is guaranteed by the unity of their methods; there are others whose unity depends upon the unity of their object. Mathematics seems to be an example of the first, while the study of languages is an example of the second. One can approach a language from the point of view of semantics. One can study its morphological aspect and its phonetics. In all three cases one has to make use of different methods, but all these approaches are linked by the unity of their subject.

It seems highly advisable to separte the problems of descriptive and of normative ethics. Only when we separate them can we see clearly what has been studied insufficiently and what has hitherto been neglected altogether. Many times writers on ethics have not kept apart questions of fact from questions of what kinds of actions are laudable and what are blameworthy. The discussions on hedonism illustrate well this point. Often the writers have made no distinction between describing a course of action and recommending it as one to be followed. An example of this is to be found in the often repeated description of morality undergoing an evolution from heteronomy to autonomy. According to this theory, man first accepted values derived from external authority, as a child does in obedience to its parents. In developing to maturity he proceeded to independent reflection, accepting some precepts and rejecting others. As a description of actual fact, this evolution from heteronomy to autonomy is unsatisfactory because most people never reach the autonomous stage. If, however, the moralist presents it, not as what is, but as what is recommended, its evaluation should be quite different. Only political rulers may object to it because sometimes people who are morally autonomous constitute difficulties for the rulers.

There is still another reason in support of at least a temporary separation of descriptive and normative ethics. Normative ethics must take into account its pedagogical effects upon people. The author must be engaged here in advocating one course of action and discouraging another. This attitude is highly dangerous for an impartial and dispassionate observer of moral life. One cannot be a good research worker if one must always keep in mind the obligation to be a good educator. Bernard Mandeville was an excellent observer of the moral life of his contemporaries and his contribution to descriptive ethics has long been underestimated. But I should not recommend his *Fable of the Bees* as a manual of normative ethics. Because of his possible influence as a moralist he has been badly treated by posterity. Only now are we able to estimate adequately his contributions to a psychology and sociology of moral life.

Some writers have pointed out that since the eighteenth century the descriptive element in books on ethics has been steadily increasing in comparison with the normative one. In fact, eighteenth-century ethical writers are very much interested in problems concerning the psychology of moral life and the problems of human nature as viewed by a moralist. But the idea of creating a separate branch of learning which would examine scientifically man's varied beliefs concerning a good life and would explain their origin, did not crystallize until the second half of the nineteenth century. One can then watch three main currents in the descriptive study of ethics. One of them is derived from Darwin and is concerned first of all with the evolution of moral ideas. I am referring to books like those of Charles Letourneau, *L'évolution de la morale* (1887), Alexander Sutherland, *The Origin and Growth of the Moral Instinct* (1898), or those of Edward Westermarck (given in footnote 17) or L. T. Houbhouse, *Morals in Evolution—A Study in Comparative Ethics* (1906). The second current is connected with the development of humanistic comparative studies in Germany. Wilhelm Wundt, in his *Ethik*, published in 1887, promised an investigation of facts and laws governing moral life (*Eine Untersuchung der Tatsachen und Gesetze des sittlichen Lebens*). Georg Simmel also planned in his *Introduction to a Science of Morals* (*Einleitung in die Moralwis-*

senschaft), published in 1892–1893, a descriptive science of moral values. Both these books contained more promises than they ever kept, being highly traditionalist in their treatment of the subject. To the same current belong, last but not least, the valuable books of Max Weber, who, especially in his *Religionssoziologie*, made an important contribution to a sociology of morals.

The third current was formed by sociologists, chiefly by Emile Durkheim and his school. Durkheim's program was developed in his work on the division of labor (*De la division du travail social*), published in 1895. As moral phenomena are social phenomena, the science which has to examine them must, according to him, belong to sociology—an opinion which would lead to the inclusion of all the humanities in sociology.

Durkheim's program of creating a so-called "physics of customs" was supported in his school by Lucien Lévy-Bruhl and, later on, by Albert Bayet. Lévy-Bruhl's well-known book *Ethics and a Science of Customs* (*La morale et la science des moeurs*), published in 1903, contained a refutation of all attacks directed against this science and very general proposals for its future development. Lévy-Bruhl agreed with his predecessor in including this branch of learning in sociology, although Durkheim's theory that a study of moral phenomena belongs to sociology because moral phenomena are social, is far from convincing. Art, literature, law, and religion are also social phenomena, but nobody would think to include in sociology any research dealing with them.

Durkheim and his school disregarded all psychological problems concerned with moral life with a contempt for psychology derived from Comte. Moritz Schlick of Vienna, in his book *Fragen der Ethik* (see footnote 11) did not notice sociological problems which could form the object of a purely descriptive and explanatory work, and proposed to insert descriptive ethics into psychology. As we have tried to show, descriptive ethics must approach its subject from different angles and take into account not only a psychology and a sociology of moral life, but also problems of meta-ethics.

By advocating the creation of an autonomous descriptive treatment of our moral life, I am not trying to depreciate normative ethics. I am watching with great interest all endeavors to build a logic of norms and I think that all kinds of deductive reasoning are quite possible in this field. If normative ethics cannot be made a science in the strict sense of the word, nevertheless it can be made more scientific than it has been. Any elucidation of concepts, any endeavor to make clear what are the fundamental norms of a given ethical system, and what can be derived from them as from premises, constitute steps toward making normative ethics more coherent. When we qualify research as scientific, we ascribe to it not a single quality, but a number of qualities subject to gradation, such as clarity, coherence, avoidance of hasty generalization, verifiability. Some of these qualities are attainable, at least to a certain degree, in normative disciplines, and the development of descriptive ethics seems very helpful for the achievement of this end.

CHAPTER II

Moral Phenomena as Dependent Variables

We are now better able to define our subject and to make clear its relation to normative and descriptive ethics. We have seen that books on ethics have discussed five groups of problems. Of these we shall not include praxiology, axiology, or felicitology in morality and therefore we shall not deal with them. The two remaining problems, social or civic morality and personal morality, we shall discuss from a descriptive and sociological point of view.

A Plea for a Sociology of Morality

The sociology of morality is not among the subjects listed in the bibliographical bulletin, *Sociological Abstracts,* and it was not discussed at six different international sociological congresses, while sociology of education, of religion, of law, were among topics discussed. The development of the sociology of morality is a topic of theoretical interest and can be of great practical importance. Only the French publication, *Année sociologique,* has from its beginning included a section on the sociology of morality, and the *Cahiers internationaux de sociologie* published a bibliography of works on the subject in 1964 (vol. 36). French interest in this problem is due to the work of Durkheim and his school. His contributions in this neglected field will be discussed later.

How can we explain this lack of interest in problems as

fascinating as these are? Are we reluctant to discuss problems so emotionally loaded and so deeply integrated into our personality? Perhaps we are skeptical as to the possibility of studying moral problems in a scientific way because of the vagueness of the concept of morality. But the concepts of religion or art or law are no less controversial. It is true that the study of religion is easier because religion usually takes institutional forms and its specialists are considered competent in matters of faith. In addition, the conspicuous variety of religious systems has been an incentive to study, while the existence of different moral systems has not been so obvious, especially for those who believe in one natural and universal morality. But the vagueness of the concept of moral values is certainly not sufficient for explaining this neglect. The concept of law is a matter of dispute which we can follow in the works of Bronisław Malinowski, for example. As to the concept of art, there was a time when the name of art was denied to motion pictures. It is not easy to tell exactly when we are entitled to count photography among the arts and when not, as would be the case of a cheap passport photograph.

In spite of the lack of research in the field of moral values, many sociologists, philosophers, and cultural anthropologist have contributed to its development with interesting observations and hypotheses. Cultural anthropologists have collected much interesting material concerning the moral life of different primitive people. But what is still lacking and very much needed is an effort at systematization. This would allow us to learn what has already been achieved and what has to be done, what hypotheses need verification, what kind of research could be organized on an international scale. I shall now review the different factors which at various times have been considered influential on the moral life of societies.

He who speaks of influences on the moral life of a society may have in mind one of the following two thoughts: First, he can mean that rule-governed behavior changes, even though the rules are still regarded as binding. For example, rules governing sexual behavior may be observed more rigorously in one period and less so in another. Second, he can mean that changes in behavior eventually change accepted rules. During the era of the Hanseatic

League, a trader who undersold other traders was regarded disdain-
fully. Daniel Defoe, a century after the decline of the League, was
still of the same opinion, respecting the solidarity of traders who
wandered from Lübeck to Novogorod tied by common danger of
robbers. Later, in the free competition of a *laissez faire* society, the
merchant whose prices were lower was regarded as the benefactor
of the consumer. The changes of conduct regulated by rules and
the changes of the rules themselves are usually interconnected.
Not only do changes in rules affect conduct but also prolonged
nonobservance of rules usually leads to their modification. Still, it
seems advisable to keep this distinction.

The Role of the Physical Environment

Although, according to the title of this book, I intend to
concentrate on social determinants of moral ideas, I should like to
mention briefly the views of writers who stressed the importance
of the physical environment for the development of man's moral
ideas and conduct.

Aristotle in Book VII, Chapter 7, of his *Politics* attributes
great importance to the climate in shaping human character:

> Those who live in a cold climate and in Europe are full of spirit,
> but wanting in intelligence and skill; and therefore they retain
> comparative freedom, but have no political organization, and
> are incapable of ruling over others. Whereas the natives of Asia
> are intelligent and inventive, but they are wanting in spirit, and
> therefore they are always in a state of subjection and slavery.
> But the Hellenic race which is situated between them is likewise
> intermediate in character, being high spirited and also intelligent.

Also communication with the sea, or lack of it, is important for
the character of citizens. People often consider that an access to
the sea is adverse to good order, because of the number of strangers brought up under other laws, and because of the mobility of
merchants coming and going, which is inimical to good government. But for safety and the provision of necessities a territory
connected with the sea is preferable.

At the end of the fourteenth century an Arabian author called
Ibn Khaldoun, who is considered one of the first sociologists,

distinguished in the world known to him seven different climates, each of them shaping man in a different way. At both extremes of the climatic ladder, people behaved, according to him, like animals, devouring each other and living without law or religion. It is a temperate climate only which gives rise to civilization. In a hot climate, he maintained, our organic tissues expand as they do under the influence of alcohol, and this is the reason why Negroes are happy and never bother about the future, while in a cold climate foresight is necessary and people are constantly hoarding provisions for an anticipated bad time.[1]

The influence of climate was particularly stressed by Montesquieu in *L'Esprit des lois*. In different climates, he argued, different needs contribute to the creation of different laws and different ways of life. In the north, people are more self-confident and thus more courageous. As they have a feeling of superiority, they are less animated by a spirit of revenge, they feel more secure and thus are more open, less likely to be suspicious, sly, or fraudulent. While in a cold climate people are not particularly apt to feel either pain or pleasure, people in hot countries are always guided by a search for pleasure, especially that provided by sexual life. Passions are here so violent that they often lead to crime. However, with the increasing heat, people grow passive, deprived of any curiosity or lofty feelings. Happiness consists for them in idleness. Difference of climate was, according to Montesquieu, decisive for the adoption of Christianity in some countries and of Islam, with its moral background, in others. He attributes to climate the existence of monogamy in some countries and polygyny, in others, polygyny being natural where women fade early and their beauty lasts only a very short time. In these conditions a need for change on the part of men seems to Montesquieu quite legitimate. Although fully aware of the numerous factors which determine the way of life of people, Montesquieu still insists on considering climate as the most important and decisive. In Book XIX he contends that "the empire of the climate is the first, the most powerful of all empires."

In agreement with Montesquieu, a French sociologist, Gaston Bouthoul, in his *Traité de sociologies*, considered it quite probable that the exhausting climate of India suggested the idea of caste in that country. A caste system absolved people of any personal effort and of any competition, because virtues and personal worth were supposed to depend on birth and not on personal merit.[2] Other writers of similar viewpoint thought that climate suggested the idea of the transmigration of souls, since this creed allowed the postponement to a future life of what one was expected to do in the present and thus provided a rationalization for indolence. Another well-known French sociologist of the Durkheim school, Marcel Mauss, demonstrated how the variations in the Eskimos' way of life depended on the change of seasons.[3] Field work was rare at the time when the school of Durkheim developed its full activity, and Mauss studied the Eskimo community by means of very rich but secondhand materials, as did Durkheim and Lévy-Bruhl when they discussed primitive peoples. Materials at the disposal of Mauss were sufficient to show that different hunting conditions in summer and in winter forced two different ways of life on the Eskimos. In summer they lived in small families dispersed throughout the hunting area; in winter they lived concentrated in a large, extended family. In summer, the father was the supreme authority of the family, while in winter the extended family was ruled by a chief. In winter, the life was socially very active, animated by many religious ceremonies, plays, and dancing. While in summer the family was strictly monogamous, during some winter ceremonies there was a general exchange of sexual partners. In their nomadic summer life the Eskimos were ruthless toward the old and sick, while during their sedentary winter life they exhibited a very gentle and protective attitude toward the weak.

With the development of sociology, the importance attributed to climatic factors lessened in favor of social determinants. As late as 1945, however, Ellsworth Huntington, of Yale University, in his book, *Mainsprings of Civilization*, stressed the importance of climate, temperature, geographic location, and diet.[4] This book stands midway between the extreme biological view and the extreme cultural or sociological view. Health and vigor are basic factors in determining the rate of human progress. Substandard diet results in stagnation. "A hot climate, especially if it is humid, makes people feel disinclined to work. This encourages the more clever people to get a living with as little physical exertion as possible. Their example fosters the growth of a social system in which hard work is regarded as plebeian." [5] Religion has been a vital factor in molding human society and, as the author tries to show, religion adjusts itself more or less to differences of geographical environment. "Small wonder then, that the Buddhist hell has six levels based on torture by heat." The finest types of religion seem to include the following, according to Huntington: "1) love, confidence and faith in place of hate, doubt and fear; 2) uniform, unbreakable law, in place of arbitrary divine interference; 3) ethical personal conduct, without which ritual and faith have little value; 4) altruism and social responsibility as the basis of social conduct." [6] The author tries to show that there exists a correlation between religious and climatic differences, regardless of whether the climate is the cause or merely an accompaniment. Among people who lack energy, merit tends to take the form of passive suffering rather than active work for others. A Hindu finds it much easier to attain holiness by lying on a bed of blunted spikes, by sitting on top of a pillar for months, or by being buried up to the neck for a while. "Heaven is merely a state of impersonal existence in which the human soul does nothing, thinks nothing, and is nothing except a part of the illimitable, quiescent soul of the universe." [7]

I quote these examples to show the trends of thought contained in this book. Huntington's claims may be questioned on two grounds. First, it is possible to find examples of people living in the same or in an analogous physical environment who have adopted different ways of life—the Pueblo Indians and the Navajos or the Eskimos and the Chukchi, for instance. Second, it is also possible to find people living under quite different conditions who have similar hierarchies of values. However, it should be noted that examples of this kind falsify only the opinion that climate is the unique determinant of human valuation, while Huntington regards climate as only one among many possible determinants of human standards.

Demographic Factors

After these remarks concerning the role played by physical environment in molding our way of life and our valuations, I should like to say a few words about the role of sex, age, the proportion of both sexes, density and growth of population, the size of the group, the mobility of its members—factors included under ecology or demography.

Let us begin with the role of sex. When we say that sex has an influence upon moral ideas expressed in norms adopted by a society or upon the conduct to which the norms refer we can mean that in one of four ways.

1. First, we may have in mind that the physical constitution of men and women affects their moral attitudes and this is in turn reflected in their conduct or valuation. Pareto considered women more compassionate and at the same time more cruel than men. Usually one attributes to men a predilection for violence and pugnacity; criminals and members of gangs of hoodlums are mostly men.

2. Second, the content of certain moral rules reveals that they were made by men rather than by women. Thus precepts recommending chastity and fidelity in women can be attributed to men because these serve man's interests. The ninth commandment of the Decalogue, "Thou shalt not covet thy neighbor's house, thou shalt not covet thy neighbor's wife, nor his manservant, nor his maidservant, nor his ox, nor his ass, nor anything that is thy neighbor's," was obviously formulated by a man who had only men's temptations in view. The legislators, usually men, have written many penal codes in which lesbianism is not mentioned or is treated with much greater tolerance than homosexuality among men. The French Declaration of 1789 was a declaration of rights of male adults. Men were expected to have the sacred right to property, while married women had to resign theirs to their husbands.

3. Third, the same act is valued differently according to whether it is performed by a man or a woman. The abandonment of a child by its mother is usually treated with much greater severity than the abandonment of a child by its father. A drunken woman is often severely condemned, while a drunken man is treated, at least in some countries, with leniency.

4. Last, the same conduct directed toward a woman can be valued differently than when it is directed toward a man. During

the German occupation in Poland the Germans did not as a rule shoot women in their weekly executions in the streets of Warsaw. Conquerors in antiquity used to enslave women and children, while men were killed. The killing of women would have been censured, as women represented no danger to the conqueror.

Similar differentiations can be made with respect to age.

1. Many authors have stressed the changes which occur in character due to age and which are accompanied by changes in moral attitudes. In Book II of his *Rhetoric*, Aristotle distinguishes youth, the prime of life, and old age:

> Young men have strong passions, and tend to gratify them in-
> discriminately. Of the bodily desires, it is the sexual by which
> they are most swayed. They are changeable and fickle in their
> desires, which are violent while they last, but quickly over: their
> impulses are keen but not deep-rooted, and are like sick people's
> attacks of hunger and thirst. They are hot-tempered and quick-
> tempered, and apt to give way to their anger; bad temper often
> gets the better of them, for owing to their love of honor they
> cannot bear being slighted, and are indignant as they imagine
> themselves unfairly treated. While they love honor, they love
> victory still more; for youth is eager for superiority over others,
> and victory is one form of this. They love both more than they
> love money. . . . Their hot temper and hopeful dispositions make
> them more courageous than older men are. . . . They would
> always rather do noble deeds than useful ones: their lives are
> regulated more by moral feeling than by reasoning. . . .
>   The character of Elderly Men . . . may be said to be formed
> for the most part of elements that are the contrary of all these.

Aristotle gives a detailed list of these elements. As for men in their prime, he deduces their characteristics rather than deriving them from observation. They are supposed to have a character between that of the young and that of the old, free from the extremes of either.[8]

2. These quotations taken from Aristotle illustrate the opin-ion that moral attitudes change with age. It is highly probable that moral rules would undergo some change if they were dictated by the young. Jean Piaget, in his book *The Moral Judgment of a Child*, distinguishes two kinds of morality: one formed in small groups composed of adults and children, that is, groups linked by

assymetrical relations and dominated by adults; the second formed in groups of children of about the same age and linked by symmetrical relations of comradeship. The first morality is a morality of constraint, domination, and unilateral respect; the second is a morality of mutual respect and cooperation. Piaget calls the first the morality of duty, and the second, the morality of goodness (*la morale du devoir et la morale du bien*). Obedience to the law, that is, generally to the authority of the adults, is typical of the morality of duty. Moral prescriptions are in this case treated verbally and obeyed with a marked tendency to conformism. The very idea of expiatory punishment is connected with the pressure of adults in family life. In fact, how would it be possible to admit that a breach of the moral law can be repaid by suffering, if this suffering is not administered by parents whom the child loves? If a child, asked by his mother to buy some bread, were punished for his neglect by being forbidden to attend a circus, he might see this prohibition as an act of revenge. But because he loves his mother, he comes to consider suffering as a justified means of reestablishing a link broken by guilt.

The idea of expiatory punishment would not occur, according to Piaget, in the minds of people brought up in groups linked by comradeship. In these groups, where mutual respect, cooperation, and equality prevail, punishment would be based on reciprocity. The boy who refused to bring bread would in turn be refused a service when he asked for it. He would not be deprived of an expected pleasure.

A morality of discipline, obedience, and conformity is, according to Piaget, represented in the works of Kant and Durkheim. All Piaget's sympathy is with the morality of peer groups of children, the morality born among equals. Rules emerging in the games of youngsters are welcomed by this great educator and his general attitude can be summed up as follows: What a pity that parents are necessary for the existence of children! In connection with this attitude, D. W. Harding in his work, *Social Psychology and Individual Values*, rightly asks why "the wish to cooperate with a pack of equals should not produce as much individual subservience as the wish to obey the elders?" [9]

Piaget's opinions, as outlined in our very brief account, stress

D

not only the importance of age for our moral attitudes, but also the importance of the relationship between people forming a group (a relation of domination and submission or a relation of equality among peers), and the importance of the existence of different generations for the formation of moral rules. In this point he was in agreement with Freud who, as everybody knows, identified conscience with the superego developed in children by the constant approval or disapproval of their elders. Piaget objected to the fact that Durkheim considered society as a homogeneous whole and did not sufficiently appreciate the role played in it by different generations.

We have noted the changes in character which advancement in age may bring about, as well as the possible effect of differences in age on moral ideas. The influence of age also reveals itself in the fact that the same conduct in a child and in an adult can be evaluated differently. The penal codes of all civilized countries establish a minimum age at which people are considered responsible for their acts and subject to certain penalties. Infants have rights but no duties. They have a right to protection. Obedience is valued positively in children and not always in adults. While truthfulness is recommended in our relations with adults, children are not always expected to be told the truth. Retired people no longer have the right to work, a right attributed to all people by the Declaration of Human Rights, adopted by the General Assembly of the United Nations in 1948.

Growing longevity can also be taken into account. "At the beginning of the Industrial Revolution," writes Vilhelm Aubert in *The Hidden Society*, "the ideal of lifelong, monogamous marriage implied, on the average, no more than to live with one's spouse for approximately seventeen years. Today it takes about forty years before death parts the spouses." [10] The present duration of marriage is a function not only of longevity but also of the fact that people marry earlier. Both these factors make the requirement of strict fidelity much more demanding.

A few words must now be said about how the relative number of men and women in a society shapes moral precepts. Montesquieu attributed polygyny not only to the influence of a climate where the attractiveness of women was short lived, but also to the fact that there were more women than men. Where, in turn, the number of men exceeded that of women we could observe, as a remedy, according to him, polyandry or male homosexuality. These old observations were recently confirmed by Lévy-Strauss in his book *Tristes tropiques*. In the Nambikwara tribe of central South America the chief has many wives. This privilege disturbs the equilibrium in the proportion of men and women, and what the natives call "sham-love," that is, male homosexuality, is practiced in compensation. In a neighboring tribe, the Tupi-Kawahib, the same privilege of the chief is balanced by polyandry.

Many cultural anthropologists recommend circumspection in relating polygamy to the ratio of men to women, as we do not have reliable statistics concerning the number of men and women in primitive societies. In 1933, Great Britain had three million more women than men, but this did not bring about the acceptance of polygyny. The Mormons however, practiced polygyny in spite of a great shortage of women. Thus the proportions of sexes seem neither sufficient nor necessary to provoke polygamy. Different factors may play a role here. Having many wives in primitive societies is often a matter of prestige, the privilege of the chief or of those who are wealthy enough to afford more than one woman.

Let us pass now to another ecological factor, the density of the population. Density of population affects our views on the legitimacy of birth control. Abortion is not condemned in overpopulated Japan and is legal. For the same reason, homosexuals are not disapproved. Density of population stimulates the creation of moral norms which assure order and cohesion in a given society, just as traffic regulations increase with the increase of cars and passengers in the streets. A dense population requires certain rules securing privacy. In the tropical forests of South America there is a primitive tribe called the Yagua. Although the entire clan lives in a single long house, the members of the large household are able to obtain privacy whenever they wish it, simply by turning their faces to the wall of the house. Whenever a man, woman, or child faces the wall, the others regard that individual as if he were no longer present.[11]

Other ecological factors which must be taken into account are the birth rate and the growth of the population. According to the well known contemporary French demographer, Alfred Sauvy, the following traits are usually correlated with a high growth potential: high mortality and a short life span, inadequate diet, a large proportion of illiterates, domination of men over women, who work only at home, child labor, absence or weakness of a middle class, lack of democracy.

David Riesman, in *The Lonely Crowd*, distinguishes three types of personality corresponding to three different demographic situations: 1) a tradition-oriented man in a society of high growth potential; 2) an inner-directed man with early internalized goals in a society of transitional population growth, and 3) an other-directed man in a society of incipient population decline.[12] These distinctions are well known and need not be discussed at length. Although the picture of these three types of personality seems convincing, I must confess that I have never been able to grasp their connection with the demographic factors mentioned above.

Not only hypotheses made by scientists but also current generalizations which cannot be ascribed to any particular author ought to be taken into account in our research. There is, for example, a common belief that high growth potential in a population is connected with little respect for life. India is often cited as an example. But, assuming that this fact is well established, this lack of respect for life may be due to the belief in rebirth.

Next to the density of the population and its growth potential, we must mention the size of a given society or of a group as one of the possible determinants of moral rules. The principle of reciprocity, considered by Malinowski as the basis for the social cohesion of the Trobriands, can work only in groups with face to face relationships. Only in groups of this kind can exist what Malinowski called a "game of give and take," a well-balanced chain of reciprocal services. This exchange differs greatly from commercial transactions. It is a ritual, initiated without expectation of gain. Services are not repaid immediately, which presupposes a sedentary life with stable personal relations. An offer of exchange of services is never refused. Both partners tend to show some generosity. Bargaining is unthinkable. Lévy-Strauss who, like Malinowski, attributes great importance to this principle of reciprocity, points out that it still functions in contemporary societies in narrow social circles, in the exchange of gifts at Christmas and on namedays and birthdays. In order to stress that this exchange is not an economic one, the gifts exchanged are not directly useful: they are usually flowers, chocolates, and the like.[13]

Mobility in space is also considered an ecological factor which is correlated with a particular way of life and hierarchies of values which include moral values. The killing of the old or the sick has always been considered connected with nomadism. We recall the Eskimos, reputed to be ruthless toward the old and sick during their nomadic summer life and protective during their sedentary winter life. In a nomadic life, children are a burden, and thus in nomadic groups fertility is not considered a blessing and birth control is not only practiced but fully admitted and even much praised.

Huntington, whom I quoted when we were considering the effects of climate, attributes to nomads a great importance in the development of civilization. "Ever since civilization became widely established," he writes, "agricultural people have vastly outnumbered pastoral nomads. Nevertheless, the nomads have repeatedly conquered and ruled the others."[14] Nomads are characterized by democracy, by which the author means, first of all, equality. Among nomads great differences in wealth are impossible. Things owned must be easily transportable. All nomad men share the same food and do the same work, as is also true among women. Mutual help is praised. Hospitality is one of their social virtues, and in fact, their survival often depends on the hospitality of others. It is a rigid requirement of their code of honor. Huntington has watched migrations among Arabs, Kurds, Kirghiz, and Mongols and has had occasion to see how initiative, quick, decisive action, and self-reliance are necessary to this kind of life. According to him, nomads must have the capacity both to lead and to follow, as raids on other nomads or on the animals of the settled people of the neighboring agricultural districts is often the only possible way to survive. These traits differ widely from those required by settled agricultural people who must be industrious but whose survival does not depend on bravery, leadership, and quick decisions. New experiences, new problems, and new responsibilities rarely confront them. In the life of the nomads the strain is great and weaklings often perish. Selective biological processes and social ideals operate simultaneously. They are reinforced by the fact that nomads usually form small groups in which intermarriage stresses the role of heredity. Huntington uses the term "kith" to refer to a group of this kind. He defines a kith as a group of people relatively homogeneous in language and culture, and freely intermarrying with one another.[15] In his opinion, kiths played a great role in our past. We have only to think of the Vikings or of the Puritans who first settled in New England.

I do not think that Huntington's theory fits all kinds of nomads and all groups which might be called kiths. Gypsies form groups relatively homogeneous in language and culture, freely intermarry with one another, and do not exhibit any enterprising traits. Living in different climates, they obstinately stick to their hierarchy of values in which labor is treated with the greatest contempt. Fortune telling, music, and theft are, at least in European countries, their principal occupations. Endeavors to make them productive and sedentary encounter great difficulties in my country. At one meeting a gypsy woman declared that life is too short to work, a statement which was very much applauded by the whole Tzigany audience. In 1952, several gypsy families were offered quite decent flats in the district of Cracow. After a short time they deserted their flats and moved into the surrounding bushes, declaring that living in flats reminded them of being in prison. The persistence of their way of life, in spite of constant migration among people of different cultures, is surprising. In France in 1960, I met a group of gypsies sitting on the grass around their Renault car. The means of transportation was new, but this was the only observable change.

In speaking of nomads we were thinking of the migration of whole groups of people. A few words must be added about the moral effect of individual migrations. Such migrations are very frequent in the United States. A French author, J. M. Domenach, in his article on the ideal pattern of man in the United States, says that in 1958, thirty-three million Americans changed their addresses.[16] According to Talcott Parsons, this mobility contributes to a restriction of the family to the nuclear one, because a mobile family cannot be numerous. In a conference held in Washington in 1960, some speakers attributed the growth of juvenile delinquency to this fact.

It is worth noting that the restriction of the family to the nuclear one can also be due to vertical mobility. When there is opportunity for advancement and when the advancement is quick, the gap between generations is great and people are sometimes embarrassed to be seen with their elders.

Alexander Gerschenkron, the well-known Harvard economist, has noted the influence of this individual mobility in space on the way people are evaluated. According to him, in migratory societies, as opposed to settled ones, the merit of people is appraised in a different way. By a "settled" society he means "one in which the whole life of an individual as a rule is passed within one fairly narrow social circle." The pre-industrial societies are an example of settled societies. In migratory, industrialized societies, a unity of life, a biography with continuity, cannot be regarded as the ideal. "The very transformation of a peasant into a city dweller, of a European into an American, create a hiatus in biography," a willingness to forget, the refusal to place a high value upon the unity of life. The value attributed to man depends on his present achievements and not on his past, where failure, crime, or humiliation could have taken place. Pre-industrial societies, according to Gerschenkron, live in the past, while industrialized societies live in the present and think of the future. They give people a chance to be reborn, which is not possible in settled societies.[17]

Alicja Iwańska, a cultural anthropologist, in her study of a community in the state of Washington, called by the fictitious name of "Goodfortune," independently confirmed the interesting observations of Gerschenkron. We read in her paper: "On the whole, Good Fortunites tend to judge one another in terms of their current activities, rather than by achievements or sins of the past. Many people 'have a skeleton in the closet' but nobody gets either too shocked or even too interested in such "skeletons.' " [18]

The Urban and the Rural Way of Life

The conviction that towns are seats of corruption is very old. The Arabian sociologist, Ibn Khaldoun, whom I cited earlier,

warned people against the perils of urban life. The rural population [in this case, nomads] contents itself easily and does not look
for sensual pleasures which only wealth can attain, while town
dwellers, having entrusted to rulers the care of their safety, lose
their resourcefulness and alertness and indulge themselves in all
possible passions.[19]

We must remember here the pastoral, the bucolic ideal of
life, abandoning culture for the sake of simplicity and truth, and
imitating a shepherd's life. Johan Huizinga, in his book *Men and
Ideas*, writes: "No other illusion has charmed humanity for so
long and with such an ever fresh splendor as the illusion of the
pining shepherd's pipe and surprised nymphs in rustling woods
and murmuring brooks. The concept is very closely akin to that of
the golden age, and constantly overlaps it: it is the golden age
brought to life." [20] The bucolic ideal was already in Theocritus of
Syracuse (about 270 B.C.) a product of urban lassitude in which
quite early the ironic tone, the awareness of lies, can be heard now
and then.

Bucolic literature, as the most perfect expression of the natural, lasted until the eighteenth century. In the age of rapid
industrialization and urbanization, at the beginning of the eighteenth century in England, Henry Fielding in his novels, especially in *The History of the Adventures of Joseph Andrews*, advocated a life far away from the turmoil of cities in which honest
people were hard to find.

Robert Redfield, in *The Primitive World and Its Transformations*, stresses the importance of urbanization for the moral order,
its importance being creative in some respects and destructive in
others. He accepts the opinion of V. Gordon Childe, who considered three events especially important in the development of
mankind: the food-producing revolution, the urban revolution,
and the industrial revolution. "After the rise of cities, men became
something different from what they had been before." Cities gave
birth to a civilization different from folk society. "We may say
that a society is civilized insofar as the community is no longer
small, isolated, homogeneous and self-sufficient; as the division of
labor is no longer simple; as impersonal relationships come to take

the place of personal relationships; as familial connections come to be modified or supplanted by those of political affiliation or contract; and as thinking has become reflective and systematic." In folk societies, moral order prevails, that is, the binding together of men consists in common conceptions as to what is right, in common ideals, in common convictions as to the good life. In cities, a technical order predominates over a moral order. "The bonds that coordinate the activities of men in the technical order do not rest on conviction as to the good life. . . . The technical order is that order which results from mutual usefulness, from deliberate coercion. . . . In the technical order men are bound by things, or are themselves things." [21]

Dealing with the effect of urban civilization on the moral order, Redfield believes that the integrity and the compelling force of the moral order in society were functions of isolation and of a slow rate of development of the technical order. Moral order flourishes when a society is shut away from outside influences. In contrast, when new ideas are rapidly introduced and people of different traditions are moving around, the moral order is thrown into confusion and its authority declines. But this would be too simple an account of the influence of urban civilization on the moral order. Urban civilization brings with it not only disorganization but also reorganization. The effects of the technical order include the creation of new moral orders. Urban life is connected with the rise of ideas as forces in history, influencing the moral order directly. Ideas become themselves causative agents in the further transformations in human living. Urban civilization brought with it such moral conflicts as could give rise to the idea of human dignity, the idea of permanent peace, or the idea of universal human responsibility. The notion of the peasant is linked to the rise of cities. The peasant is a rural native whose long established order of life takes important account of the city: an economic, political, and moral account. The existence of the art of reading and writing has become an element of his mode of life, although he himself may not read or write. [22] He compares himself with city dwellers and in industry, physical endurance, honesty, and sexual morality thinks himself superior. The concept of peasant makes sense only in reference to the town. The Navajo, according to Redfield, are not peasants. Peasants represent a mixture of the moral and technical order.[23]

The Role of Industrialization

Since the publication of Redfield's book in 1953, volumes have been written on the processes of industrialization and urbanization which we can watch at present in different countries of the world. I shall limit myself to a brief account of surveys done in my country concerning changes in the way of life of Polish peasants who come into town to work in industry.

Before the present intense industrialization, the family life of our peasants was characterized by male domination, by the father's supremacy. There was a strict division of labor between the peasant and his wife. Children were completely dependent economically on their elders as the possessors of the land. They had to put up with it as they had no alternative. They were dependent on their parents in the choice of their partners in marriage. This long period of dependence led to infantilization.

Now the family life of peasants is radically changed. When the father works in industry, his wife must assume many of his duties, including those which had never been assigned to a woman before. She is overworked, but her position in the family is much stronger. Her husband, after returning from town, sometimes helps her in duties previously given only to women, such as care of the poultry. Possession of land has ceased to be the only measure of personal prestige. Education has become more important. The contact with towns has contributed to the rationalization of farming methods. When land was cultivated in a traditional way, the only possibility for advancement was to buy more land. Now contact with industry suggests advancement through intensification of production and better education. The young sons of peasants who move to town are liberated from the constant control of their neighbors. Their work has time limits and they are free to do what they choose after their daily work is finished. They have a free choice of the milieu in which they spend their leisure time. Their mobility, horizontal as well as vertical, is much greater.

These new conditions have changed their way of life from a rural to an urban one. For these changes, urbanization is mainly responsible, while industrialization simply leads to urbanization. Of course, I do not contend that industrialization combined with urbanization are the only factors which make for this change. Everybody knows that mass media must also be taken into account as a means by which urban life reaches the most remote villages. In the underdeveloped countries of Africa or South America, where the processes of urbanization and industrialization do not go hand in hand but where urbanization precedes industrialization, the changes in ways of life are different. The rural population moves into town, and with no chance of finding a job, becomes a *lumpenproletariat*.

As was said above, many changes attributed to industrialization are only indirectly dependent on it. But there are changes in ways of life which can be directly attributed to the development of industry. William Hogarth, the eighteenth-century English painter, was a man of modest means, but he had six servants. We know this from his picture of his own household. As a rule, servants were recruited from a surplus of rural population. In industrialized countries there is no surplus rural population and servants are rare and expensive. In connection with this fact, historians point to the decline of social parties with a quantity of dishes, the decline of a festival culture which can still be observed in the diary of Samuel Pepys.

The processes of industrialization going on in different countries at the present time suggest the possibility of initiating comparative research on their moral effects. It would, for example, be interesting to learn what the moral effects are in countries which adopt Euro-American technology along with the Western way of life and in countries where the technology of advanced countries is accepted while their morality is not. Contemporary China imitates the West in her efforts to develop atomic weapons, but she rejects bourgeois culture and its morality as well as her own tradition. Other countries accept Western technology and at the same time glorify their own tradition and hierarchy of values.[24]

The role of industrialization is closely related to the role of technical inventions. This role is well known and we can content ourselves with a few examples. The invention of gunpowder was one of the multiple factors which contributed to the decline of chivalry and its code of fair play. This code was made for knights engaging in face to face combat. Now the enemy can be reached from a distance and the manipulation of gunpowder is accessible to everybody and requires little skill. Modern means of transportation enable people to have contact with systems of values different from their own and this contributes to a revision of their own valuations and promotes tolerance. The decline of parental authority over children has often been attributed to quick technical development. A grandmother who has never flown in an airplane cannot be expected to exercise great authority over children fascinated by modern technology. The extension of leisure time due to scientific inventions brings a considerable change in the way of life. The use of constantly improving contraceptives is connected with a great change in sexual life and sexual ethics. Owing to new discoveries in medicine, the physician faces entirely new ethical problems, for example, the legitimacy of using treatments which change the personality of a patient, or of keeping alive at great cost someone whose brain is severely damaged.

Economic Determinants

Let us dwell a little longer upon economic determinants, to which I alluded when speaking of industrialization. We speak of determinants in the plural because the so-called economic factor is of course a complicated set of possible independent variables. They include the standard of living, the kind of production, the techniques of production, human relations in production, the distribution of wealth. It is not always easy to distinguish between the roles of economic and ecological factors and to tell which of them are immediate causes and which belong to more remote conditions in the causal chain. The climate may influence an ideology directly: Montesquieu, we remember, attributed the ideal of nirvana to the climate of India. But climate can influence ideals through its influence on the methods of securing subsistence. Very often it is a matter of pure convention, whether we attribute certain social phenomena to economic or to ecological causes.

Engels considered production as the last link in the causal chain, but nobody can grow cotton in Greenland. "The differences of mores and institutions of different peoples," wrote Ibn Khaldoun, "depend on the way in which people secure their subsistence." [25] This quotation sounds almost like an avowal of Marxist historical materialism. Repeating the same idea almost word for word, Montesquieu wrote, "Laws are closely connected with the way in which different peoples secure their subsistence." But laws, according to him, depend on needs and needs are determined by climate. The inhabitants of Marseille had to resort to commerce because the soil they lived on was sterile. They had to be diligent in order to compensate for unfavorable natural conditions. They had to be honest in order to deal successfully with the barbarous countries that surrounded them. [26]

Discussing the role of economic factors in connection with Marxist historical materialism, the Belgian sociologist, Eugène Dupréel, pointed out two main senses in which the economic factor has been spoken of. 1) In the first, restricted, sense we have to include in the domain of economic factors all activities aiming at the satisfaction of elementary biological needs. 2) In the second and very broad sense we include all activities which affect, even indirectly, our own or other people's elementary needs. In the last sense, the activity of the small farmer who assures himself and his family some means of subsistence, as well as the activity of the millionaire who adds new millions to those he already possesses, are termed economic. This last sense is broad enough to include almost all kinds of human activity. According to Dupréel, when Marxists consider economic factors fundamental, they have usually the first, narrow sense in mind, while when they stress their universal presence, they think of the second. The universal presence of economic determinants cannot be shown if we take the restricted sense into account, while the thesis concerning the economic factors as fundamental does not seem convincing when one speaks of economic factors in the large sense. [27]

I cannot dwell any longer on the conceptual difficulties connected with the word "economic." My remarks are aimed only at pointing out the complications involved in this category. Neither will I try to exhaust all possible connections between economic phenomena and moral phenomena, but refer only to a few examples.

Long ago people stressed the connection between poverty and the difficulty of living up to moral requirements. *Not kennt kein Gebot,* proclaimed a well known German proverb, meaning that in necessity you cannot expect a respect for prohibitions. Hesiod in his *Works and Days* stressed the connection between virtue and wealth. Everybody knows Benjamin Franklin's dictum that it is hard for an empty sack to stand upright.

"Poverty creates a subculture of its own. One can speak of the culture of the poor, for it has its own modalities and distinctive social and psychological consequences for its members," writes Oscar Lewis, the cultural anthropologist, who has written several books about Mexico City. "It seems to me that the culture of poverty cuts across regional, rural-urban, and even national boundaries." [28] "The culture of poverty is a way of life, remarkably stable and persistent, passed down from generation to generation along family lines." [29]

This subculture is characterized by the following traits: lack of privacy, gregariousness, alcoholism, frequent use of physical violence by men toward their wives and children, free sexual unions, frequent abandonment of mothers and children, early initiation into sex, emphasis upon family solidarity, a trend toward mother-centered and matrilocal families, but male superiority, a cult of masculinity called *machismo* (the word refers to sexual exploits in the higher strata of the population and means heroism and lack of fear in the lower), a general attitude marked by resignation and fatalism.

Among the economic traits Lewis notices are: a constant struggle for survival, unemployment and underemployment, low wages for a miscellany of unskilled occupations, child labor, the absence of savings, a chronic shortage of cash, the absence of food reserves in the house and frequent buying of small quantities of food (children are sent many times a day for small purchases), the pawning of personal goods, borrowing from lenders at usurious rates of interest, credit organized spontaneously by neighbors, the use of secondhand clothing and furniture.

As to the political and religious attitudes of the poor, Lewis stresses their mistrust of government and those in high positions, their mistrust of hospitals and doctors, their hatred of the police and the administration of justice, their mistrust of labor unions, and their feeling of marginality. A member of this culture is attached to the ritual side of religion, but does not think very much of priests. Marriage in church is respected as opposed to civil marriage, but it is rather rare as there is nothing to inherit and the question of legacy does not intervene.

The attitude of resignation and apathy mentioned by the author manifests itself in a complete absence of any aspiration for advancement. Of the five children of Sanchez only one, a girl named Consuelo, tries to become better educated than the rest of her family. Unfortunately she is exploited by men and does not succeed in her endeavor.

The subculture characterized by Lewis is typical of unskilled workers who live on the margin of a big city. It is not the culture of poverty in general. The way of life of poor peasantry is different and so is the ethos of many poor primitive people. A déclassée middle class does not create a culture of poverty. The attitudes of the people described by Lewis depend on the existence of a social stratification. These people know of the existence of those who use department stores, city banks, museums, art galleries, and airports, but they do not regard these privileges as theirs. They feel themselves to be on the bottom and consider any endeavor to rise to be hopeless. Such resignation does not exist when people have no higher strata above their heads when they do not feel like the underdogs. Only when the culture Lewis describes is taken to be the way of life of a lumpenproletariat does it "cut across regional and even national boundaries." His picture constitutes an ideal type in the sense of Max Weber. It can be fully realized or realized only partially.

A continuous struggle for existence certainly affects the moral ideas of people in many ways. Different kinds of homicide are accepted by the Eskimos. Invalids, the sick, and the old are doomed to death. Newborn girls are often left to freeze outside the igloo because girls are less effective in securing food. If twins are born, the weaker shares the same fate. There is a tendency to attribute the character of the Dobu to their great poverty. "Life in

Dobu," writes Ruth Benedict in *Patterns of Culture*, "fosters extreme forms of animosity and malignancy which most societies have minimized by their institutions. Dobuan institutions, on the other hand, exalt them to the highest degree." According to the Dobuan view of life, "virtue consists in selecting a victim upon whom he can vent the malignancy he attributes alike to human society and the powers of nature. . . . Suspicion and cruelty are his trusted weapons in his strife and he gives no mercy, as he asks none. . . . The Dobuan . . . is dour, prudish and passionate, consumed with jealousy and suspicion and resentment." [30] These traits, as well as the fierce exclusiveness of ownership, may be attributed in part to the extreme harshness of Dobuan life. On the other hand, Lévi-Strauss in *Tristes tropiques* describes the Nambikwara tribe in the central part of Latin America as full of good will, benevolence, and readiness to laugh and play, although they are doomed to hunger in the dry season.

Although poverty and affluence clearly affect moral ideas and behavior, it is not a simple matter to say exactly how they do so. We can only add this subject to our list of those which need further exploration.

From the quantity of goods we can pass to their quality. The American anthropologist, Alfred Louis Kroeber, made the rather sad remark that there is a correlation between how quickly the goods a society produces deteriorate and its practice of hospitality. We are less hospitable when the goods we have are durable than when they are not, or when the existence of money enables the owner to sell them eventually. "The moment food and shelter must be purchased," Kroeber wrote, "the hospitality of savages becomes out of question." [31] Where goods are durable, we can store them up for different reasons. We may do it for security. Also we may do it for prestige: sometimes because of the scarcity of provisions and sometimes because of our readiness to destroy what we possess, as in the case of the potlatch of the Kwakiultl.

A specialist in the history of religion has suggested that in ancient Iran the dualism of the right and the wrong was developed by agricultural tribes, who learned to produce food and breed animals. For an agricultural tribe, the land was divided into fertile and sterile, animals into domesticated and wild, people into cultivators and barbarians. This dualistic mode of thinking was manifested in a dualistic religion which distinguished between benevolent gods and fiendish demons.[32]

Some authors attribute the position of women to the extent to which they take part in acquiring the means of subsistence, which in turn depends on what is produced. Whenever gardening constitutes the main form of production, women, having a greater share in this kind of work, are expected to acquire a better position in the community. This in turn affects moral norms and particularly those which concern sexual life and the family. Many contemporary writers have pointed to the fact that changes in our moral opinions on the legitimacy of slavery were due to a change in the techniques of production which made slavery unprofitable. Human relations in production connected with class interests may provide an explanation for the fact that the Puritans, who required chastity of white women, permitted sexual promiscuity among their black workers. All these factors are closely related to class distinctions and class interests, whose role as determinants of moral ideas will be treated later on.[33]

Differences in type of production may partially account for differences in morality observed among pastoral mountain dwellers and agricultural plainsmen. One of contemporary Polish sociologists devoted several years to the study of these differences, comparing the way of life of Polish mountain dwellers of the Tatras with that of their immediate neighbors on the plains. Our mountain dwellers exhibit an ethic of honor, self-distinction, and magnanimity whose superiority is admitted by the inhabitants of the plains. It is not easy to decide what is due here to pastoral life and what to the fact that our mountain dwellers, owing to their geographic location, were never confined to serfdom.

The Division of Labor and Morality

We shall now pass to another subject, namely, the influence exercised on morality by the division of labor. As this influence has often been discussed, we shall dwell on this subject a little longer. Bernard Mandeville, in Dialogue IV of his *Fable of the Bees*, was the first, so far as I know, to note that the division of labor, by making men dependent on one another, played an important and positive role in the development of morality. This positive influence was stressed later on by Adam Smith in the first chapter of his *Wealth of Nations*. However, the first person to develop this subject at length was Emile Durkheim in his book called *De la division du travail social*, published in 1893.

Durkheim acknowledges that he is not the first to speak of the importance of the division of labor for the development of morality, but he is the first to distinguish two kinds of solidarity, one of them being the function of growing professional specialization.

In primitive societies, according to Durkheim, all members repeat the same kind of activities and are self-sufficient in their production. Everyone cultivates his own land, builds his own hut, makes his own garments. This gives rise to a solidarity born of similarity. Durkheim calls this solidarity *mechanic*. Another kind of solidarity is connected with professional differentiation. In a society where labor is divided, people depend on one another and solidarity is fostered by their interests. This kind of solidarity is called *organic*. One can measure its degree by observing how laws function in a given community. According to Durkheim, where law is enforced by means of repressive sanctions, solidarity is mechanic; it is organic in societies where breach of law is followed by indemnities secured by a contract. As contracts presuppose some kind of equality among the partners, the growth of the division of labor is connected with the growth of equality and at the same time with the growth of personal autonomy and individuality. Social cohesion is thus realized because of the fact that people are different and not in spite of it.

This equilibrium can be achieved, however, only when the division of labor is a sound division, that is, when everybody is free to choose his profession and when the external conditions of the social struggle are equal.

It is not possible to discuss here all the arguments of different writers against Durkheim's theory. Malinowski long ago criticized the supposed similarity of peoples in primitive societies and showed convincingly that at least in some of these societies—for example, among the Trobriands—laws based on reciprocity are of fundamental importance for the life of the cummunity, while repressive law, corresponding to our criminal law, is, in contradiction to Durkheim's view, very rarely used. Certainly, neither is it true that laws fixing mutual obligations presuppose equality. Neither the laws concerning exchanges of services between the chief of a primitive community and its members, nor the laws concerning exchange of services between the lord and the serfs in a feudal society are laws binding two equal partners. Their equality consists solely in having an equal duty to keep their respective obligations.

Finally, one has to add to these objections the fact that the division of labor does not necessarily work for equality because different professions are usually given different social rank. For centuries manual work has been regarded in the Western world as degrading: in England even in Dickens' time, surgeons were not admitted into society and the same was true of dentists, because they worked with their hands. There was also further stratification among manual workers. In many countries farmers have been particularly despised. The oldest division of labor was probably according to sex, and this division was associated very early with contempt for the work done by women. It was degrading for a man to assume the work of a woman. Thus the assumption that the division of labor results in equality does not seem convincing. In many countries it is only very recently that because of their wives' professions outside the home men have agreed to share in the housework and to share in looking after the children. A man pushing a baby carriage in the street or working in the garden is not a rare sight nowadays.

Professional Differentiation as a Factor in the Differentiation of Morality

Durkheim believed that professional differentiation was supposed to work toward social cohesion. But the question arises, whether social cohesion, due to mutual interdependence, was not troubled by the fact that each profession developed a moral code of its own, which could threaten the monolithic character of Durkheim society and the harmony built upon dissimilarity.

Many authors have written about professional ethics, but few have asked how much the ethics of one profession differs from that of another and from the ethic generally recommended in a given society and taught in its elementary schools.

The ethics of some professions differ from the generally accepted morality of a society only in degree or in the emphasis put on particular duties. Medical ethics can be cited as an example. Ever since Hippocrates elaborated a code binding in the medical profession, physicians have been expected to keep confidential some information given them by their patients. Keeping secret what is known confidentially is expected from everybody, but it is particularly expected of a physician who must have the trust of his patient in order to diagnose and cure his illness and who has unusual occasions for hearing confidences. The physician's code also binds him to use his knowledge only for the good of the people he deals with. This too is generally recommended but is especially emphasized for a physician who is in an unusual position to do harm. In the same way nobody is expected to give false information, but a teacher is expected to be particularly careful in correctly informing his pupils. In these examples there is a quantitative difference between the rules for the profession and those generally accepted; it is a difference of emphasis rather than one of content.

The situation seems different for commerce. Writers of the seventeenth and eighteenth centuries, who wished to praise the social function of the middle class, were unanimous in asserting the benevolent influence of commerce. According to them, trade fostered the exchange of knowledge among peoples of different cultures, teaching them to understand one another and to look at their own customs from an outsider's point of view. Peoples were thus made more tolerant, while awareness of their mutual dependence in the exchange of goods made them peace-loving. It is a general rule, wrote Montesquieu, that in countries where people are customarily kind we find a developed trade. It cannot be denied, he concedes, that trading people are rarely hospitable and seldom develop altruistic virtues, but we owe to the spirit of trade the development of a sense of justice against a tendency to violence and plunder.[34]

In spite of this eulogy of commerce repeated by many eighteenth century writers, some of them were perfectly aware of a contradiction existing between rules governing trade and the teachings of Christianity. "Religion is one thing and trade is another," wrote Mandeville in *The Fable of the Bees*. If trade observed moral rules it would, he said, never flourish, and in this conflict of rules, trade has always been victorious. "Bargaining has neither friends nor relations," wrote Benjamin Franklin. The famous saying, "business is business" was quoted later on to justify practices admissible in trade but disapproved outside this profession. This contradiction between rules governing trade and rules recommending us to have the good of our neighbor first in mind, was made explicit by John Atkinson Hobson in his book *Wealth and Life: A Study in Values*, published in London in 1929. "Take as much as you can, and give as little as you can," was, in his opinion, the rule which governed trade and which was repudiated by the moralist. Merchants apply Hobson's principle without guilt and without censure, thus we have to note here not only a type of conduct but also a set of rules governing a profession which are at odds with those governing society as a whole.

Durkheim, who thought that a division of labor had integrative effects, pointed out himself a conflict between the professional code of a soldier and that of a scientist. The first is expected to be obedient to his superiors, while distrust of any authority is the moral duty of a scientist.

The code of politicians was among the first to raise objections from moralists. Socrates, in the *Apology*, acknowledged that he was warned by his daimonion not to take part in politics if he wanted to defend the right cause successfully. D'Alembert complained that the morality of politicians who control relations between states was still on the level of the morality of individuals in the state of nature, where conflicts could be resolved only by force.[35] David Hume in Volume II, Book 3, of his *Treatise of Human Nature*, acknowledged that "there is a system of morals calculated for princes, concerning the laws of Nations much more free than that which ought to govern private persons." He explained the relaxation of morality in international affairs by the fact that the obligations among individuals are much more important for the life of the community than obligations among different states and thus, he concluded, "we must necessarily give a greater indulgence to a prince or minister who deceives another, than to a private gentleman who breaks his word of honor."

Insofar as politicians and statesmen justify such measures as espionage, deceit, and breach of agreement as painful necessities in the face of similar measures adopted by their opposite numbers, we are not dealing with new moral rules but with the transgression of rules already accepted by both politicians and by our society in general. The situation changes, however, when a statesman considers himself fully justified in doing things which would be censured in private relations, because he is acting not for himself, but for the common good. Cavour, the Italian statesman, was famous for having said that he would be a scoundrel if he did for himself things which he did for Italy. In their role as guardians politicians consider themselves entitled to deceive the public, to make alliances with people they despise, to attain success by any means. Their first priority is power and in order to secure this they must manipulate people. Lord Chesterfield, who wanted his son to go into politics, recommended to him, in his letter of 15 January 1748, the following:

> An absolute command of your temper, so as not to be provoked to passion upon any account; patience to hear frivolous, impertinent and unreasonable applications; with address enough to refuse without offending; or, by your manner of granting, to double the obligation; dexterity enough to conceal a truth, without telling a lie; sagacity enough not to let them discover anything by yours—a seeming frankness with a real reserve. These are the rudiments of a politician.[36]

While politicians try to defend their moral code by contending that they are forced into it as guardians of the public weal, some professions justify their transgressions of moral precepts by referring to the conditions in which these professions are exercised. Members of the landed gentry were often accused of being irresponsible in meeting their engagements. The answer to this charge was that the soil was unreliable. A prolonged drought or a rain could ruin all calculations and make it impossible to deliver in due time what one had promised. In this case both the accuser and the accused are asked to recognize the limitations within which moral rules can be applied, while the code of politicians even contains precepts which are in flagrant contradiction to those fostered by moralists.

Before I close this section on the role of economic factors in moral attitudes of people, I should like to mention the effects of the way in which goods are distributed. In his book *The Freudian Ethic: An Analysis of the Subversion of American Character*, (published in New York in 1959), Richard T. La Piere deplores the death of the Puritan ethic in contemporary America. By the Puritan ethic he means an ethic which approves of initiative, personal responsibility, enterprise, stubbornness in realizing one's goals, frugality, discipline, and readiness to renounce present comfort for the sake of the future. Multiple and interdependent factors are contributing to this change. I shall return later to some of them. But what is of interest here is the buying and selling of goods on the installment plan. In the time of Benjamin Franklin one had to save money in order to buy expensive things. It was a good way to practice self-discipline. In his autobiography Franklin relates how long he had to postpone the luxury of eating from china imported from the Far East. Nowadays a recently married couple begins by buying a refrigerator, a radio, or a television set. The sum due will be paid eventually, but the discipline needed in order to pay the debt is no longer self-discipline but a discipline imposed from above. This way of selling merchandise promotes the tendency to enjoy life first, to indulge oneself, and to renounce nothing.

The examples given above will be, I hope, sufficient to show how varied and numerous are the economic factors which can play a role in shaping our moral attitudes. I have not taken into account the role of class economic interests as I intend to speak of them at length later on.

Political Factors: The Type of Government

Eighteenth-century writers stressed particularly the importance of the form of government for the development of the moral life of the governed. Among them was Montesquieu, who saw the evils of monarchy and prophesied a great change for the better in a republic.

Montesquieu divided the main forms of government into three types: 1) the monarchy ruled with respect for the laws; 2) despotism, that is, the rule of one man, but without regard for the law; 3) the republic, which could have an aristocratic or a democratic form.

The ruler in a monarchy, in Montesquieu's sense, and the despotic ruler, each for his own sake foster quite different moral attitudes among their subjects. Social hierarchy is absolutely indispensable to the existence of monarchy. In order to back up social distinctions, monarchy must constantly recur to the concept of honor and provoke an interplay of ambitions extorting from people sacrifices motivated merely by the desire for renown.

While monarchy must excite ambition, despotism rules by fear. No one can here set himself above others. All must be equal in their slavery. In order to make good slaves out of people, a despot must begin by making them bad citizens. It is only in the republic that civic virtues flourish, because they are absolutely indispensable for its maintenance.

In countries ruled by means of coercion one can observe a constant conflict between obedience and dignity:

> Such a conflict, if it does not result in a protest, leads to an adjustment of the sense of dignity to the conditions imposed. In some individuals this consists in a change in one's own convictions. In succumbing to coercion the individual tries to believe that what he is required to do is a just thing. In other individuals the retention of convictions is accompanied by a tendency to belittle the importance of the behavior enforced; If such enforced behavior is symbolic in nature, attempts are, as a rule, made to emphasize the conventional character of that behavior and to give it a different meaning. If such behavior is not merely conventional, conformism is often justified by the assertion that what is sacrificed is less important than that to which it is sacrificed, in other words, it is claimed that higher values are preserved by one's succumbing to coercion. . . . On the social scale, strong external coercion results in a polarization of psychological types into opportunism and the psychology of submission on the one hand and the psychology of rebellion and heroism, on the other.[37]

The effects of political coercion were long ago described by Aristotle. A despotic ruler, according to him, must be on his guard against anything which is likely to inspire either courage or confidence among his subjects; he must prohibit literary assemblies or other meetings for discussion. A tyrant should also endeavor to know what each of his subjects says or does and should employ spies, for the fear of informers prevents people from speaking their minds, and if they do, they are more easily found out. Another art of the tyrant is to sow quarrels among the citizens. The tyrant is also fond of making war in order that his subjects may have something to do and be always in want of a leader. Tyrants are always fond of bad men because they love to be flattered and no man who has the spirit of a freeman in him will lower himself by flattery. It is characteristic of a tyrant to dislike everyone who has dignity or independence.

Aristotle considers that all he said above could be summed up under three heads. The tyrant aims at the humiliation of his subjects, as he knows that a meanspirited man will not conspire against anybody. He aims at the creation of mistrust among them and is at war with the good because they are loyal to one another and do not inform against one another. The tyrant desires that his subjects be powerless as they will not attempt to overthrow tyranny if they are incapable of action.[38]

Modern despotism has many analogies with ancient despotism as described by Aristotle, but it has also some features of its own. Seneca, under the reign of Nero, adopted the doctrine of the Stoics. Would this philosophy suit the time of Stalin? I do not think so. Why not? The main thesis of the Stoics was that nobody can deprive us of our moral values and therefore moral values are the only ones which deserve our attention and our attachment. You can be put into jail, they kept repeating, you can be sent into exile, but nobody can deprive you of the possibility of being a man of virtue. This conviction, which constituted the basic principle of the Stoic ethic, has been shaken in the time of concentration camps where new methods, often successful, have been used to break the human spirit.

We have today many descriptions of measures undertaken to

achieve this end. I shall refer here only to the book of Bruno Bettelheim entitled *The Informed Heart,* published in 1960. The author gives a detailed account of the methods and effects of coercion in the concentration camps of Buchenwald and Dachau. The initial shock to which the prisoner was submitted was that of being torn away from his family, friends, occupation, and social position, from his status. The prisoner was deprived of his name and given a number. Soon he was led to give up his individuality, so as to have a better chance of survival. Not to be noticed, to disappear in the crowd—this kind of behavior proved sensible. Prisoners were methodically debased by being treated like children, by being forced to do stupid work like digging holes in the ground with their bare hands, although tools were available. They were degraded by being forced to curse their God and to accuse themselves of vile actions. Heroism which could be the highest assertion of individuality was prevented by the fact that the whole group had to suffer for it. Thus the group came to resent heroism, instead of admiring and respecting the hero.

The Role of Bureaucracy

I have discussed the effects of certain political factors on the morality of the ruled and more particularly the effect of coercion, most conspicuous in extreme situations like those in concentration camps. Now I would like to mention the effect of centralization of power in a contemporary state. I must refer here to the well known book of W. H. Whyte, *The Organization Man.* The centralization of power in a contemporary state is correlated with the growth of bureaucracy. Bureaucracy favors a new model of man, a new ideal of personality, which Whyte calls the well-rounded man. I expect that the image of the well-rounded man is widely known and so I shall not dwell any longer upon it. We remember that, according to this author, the growing role of organization in modern societies is connected with the growth of an organization ideology which in turn promotes a social ethic called by Whyte an organization or bureaucratic ethic. Let me quote his main characterization of this kind of ethic. "By social ethic I mean that contemporary body of thought which makes morally legitimate the pressures of society against the individual. Its major propositions are three: a belief in the group as the source of creativity; a belief in 'belongingness' as the ultimate need of the individual; and a belief in the application of science to achieve the belongingness." [39] In this ethic, independence is no longer a respected value. "These days you must do what somebody else wants you to do," and this fact is not treated as a painful necessity. The organization man denies that there is any conflict between the individual and the society. He imagines himself living in a benevolent atmosphere. As he is well rounded he does his best to make the lives of others pleasant. His world is harmonious and safe, at least for mediocrities.

A quite different effect of the growing bureaucracy on the individual is represented by several contemporary novelists. As the most striking example we may cite Franz Kafka and his books *The Trial* and *The Castle*. There is here a conflict between the individual and the society. Bureaucracy, including its legal apparatus, oppresses the individual who is struggling hopelessly with an anonymous power. It is fear that dominates him and not a comfortable feeling of safety due to what Whyte calls "togetherness." The same conflicts are found in the works of Dürrenmatt and Frisch.

The Influence of Social Stratification

I should like to consider now the influence of social stratification upon the morality of a given society. This influence can be manifold.

1. The very fact of the existence of a stratification, whatever its basic principle may be, can effect the moral life of a society. For example, the Belgian philosopher, Eugène Dupréel, thinks that the existence of a social hierarchy can promote the development of a kind of virtues which he calls "honorific" or *vertus d'honneur*, which he distinguishes from "virtues of benevolence" or *vertus de bienfaisance*. Honorific virtues are connected with personal excellence. People aspire to them in order to reach an ego-ideal and distinguish themselves from the vulgar. As these virtues serve this purpose they cannot be easy to acquire. They need effort and

renunciation. In opposition to them, the so-called virtues of benevolence are concerned with human welfare and work for the happiness of the people. The effort of the agent is here irrelevant and the emphasis is put on the effect of one's actions. We remember that David Hume, in his *Principles of Morals,* criticized the ascetic virtues manifested in fasting, sexual chastity, and so on, showing that their only result was to make those who practiced them sour and disagreeable. In the light of Dupréel's distinction, as I have already pointed out in my first chapter, this criticism was due to a misunderstanding: ascetic virtues are practiced not in order to be pleasant or helpful to other people, but in order to reach an ideal of personal excellence. This excellence was particularly stressed by people belonging to the higher strata of the social ladder—a fact expressed in the well-known saying, *noblesse oblige,* privilege entails responsibility.

Dupréel's opinion that a stratified society gives birth to moral emulation, connected with a respect for virtues not easy to acquire, presupposes that the social hierarchy is not once and forever stabilized, as in a caste system, but that a person can cross social barriers on his own merits. The classes situated lower down the social ladder may prove by their excellence that they deserve to move higher, while the upper classes may, referring to their own moral excellence, justify their privileged position, especially at a time when it is threatened. The privileged have a justified fear of those who are below, not only when they threaten them, but also when they admire them and wish to emulate and to join them. It would be interesting to see what consequences for moral life social stratification may have where there is no possibility for advancement, social position being, as in the caste system, determined forever by birth.

2. There is another aspect to the problem of the influence of social stratification on morality. Social stratification can affect our moral life in the sense that moral prescriptions or proscriptions may differ when they refer to people belonging to different social classes. In Poland until the end of the eighteenth century the killing of a peasant by a man belonging to the gentry was punished by demanding a small pecuniary compensation. A man who killed another of his own class was sentenced to death. Theft committed

by a Brahmin in India is much more severely condemned than theft committed by someone belonging to a lower caste. In both cases the influence of social stratification on morality is manifested by a differentiation in approval and disapproval, according to the position of the agent as well as the position of the person who is the object of his action. Different ideals are also often accepted in ethical systems for people belonging to different classes, some people being considered as born to rule, and others as born to obey.

3. The third and most common way of speaking of the influence of class distinctions on morality is to point out that each class has a moral system of its own. Thorstein Veblen, in his book *The Theory of the Leisure Class,* first published in 1899, gave us a picture of the ethos of the upper classes, while other writers have spoken of bourgeois morality or of the morality of the proletarians. By proletarian morality they understood sometimes a morality born in a proletarian milieu, sometimes a morality adopted by proletarians, although born outside their class, or, finally, the morality which proletarians should adopt if they were sufficiently class conscious. The same ambiguities could be noted in the concept of a middle class morality. It could be a morality born in this class, one adopted by it, or one best suited to its vital interests.

Dupréel noted one possible moral effect of belonging to the highest stratum of a social hierarchy. Members of this class require more of themselves just because they are the privileged and more is expected of them by others. As I mentioned before, the Brahmins in India were more severely treated if they stole than those who belonged to a lower caste. But in a society stratified into the rich and the poor, one can watch another moral effect of belonging to the privileged—the tendency to justify one's privileges by rationalization. In eighteenth-century France Baron Holbach, a very wealthy man, could sincerely believe that the existence of rich people is a blessing for the poor because the rich provide the poor with work. The poor in turn are needed by the rich to do the work they would not like to do themselves. Therefore the existence of the rich and the poor was the best possible arrangement and due to a benevolent Providence. In Holbach's opinion there was no reason to envy the rich because the poor had fewer troubles and thus a greater chance to be happy. Holbach did not see the contradiction between this opinion and another he upheld, that death was a milder experience for a poor man than a rich man because the former had less to lose.

Today, soothing one's conscience by such considerations would hardly be possible. Still, some privileged people have a tendency to believe that their privileges are deserved rewards for their merits or that one can be as happy living in a slum as in a luxurious house.

Social stratification is not always based on economic criteria. Max Weber pointed out groups whose hierarchy was based on status. The privileged were, in this case, characterized by a way of life of their own, which was not easy to adopt but which was necessary for anyone wishing to belong to their group. They usually despised economic activity, manual labor, and artistic achievements connected with manual work, such as sculpture. Brahmins conspicuously manifested their contempt for any activity aiming at gain and, according to Weber, the more the group was economically threatened by those who were below, the more it was opposed to the parvenus, to the newcomer. The children of these newcomers could be accepted only if they were educated in the same conventions and did not stain their good reputations by any business activity. Strata distinguished by economic criteria are characterized first of all by their relation to production, while those distinguished by status are characterized in terms of consumption. Those privileged by status usually exploit their past to justify their present position, while the attitude of those of lower class is directed toward the future. The privileged often believe that God has endowed them with a mission or calling.

Role and Morality

We pass now to a very important factor, completely disregarded, so far as I know, in the formulation of moral commandments which are so often phrased in a general way without the necessary differentiations. I dealt with this factor when I mentioned the differentiation brought about by different professions. To be a physician or a lawyer is to play a role which arouses certain expectations and to which a set of duties is related. A physician is condemned for refusing his help in an urgent case. A teacher is expected to tell the truth. But roles change not only with professions. There is the role of an employer and an employee, the role of a father, or a son or of a daughter, the role of a host and his visitors, the role of a deputy, the role of a goalkeeper, of a bridegroom, of a president, of a master and his servant, of a public prosecutor and a defense lawyer, and so on.

In case of a shipwreck, the captain is expected to be the last to leave his ship. A diplomat is not expected to be sincere, while sincerity is required of a friend. Sons are given a right to emancipation earlier than daughters. They are given a higher degree of privacy. Daughters are held to a more exacting code of filial and kinship obligations and parents expect from them more protection when they are old than they do from their sons.[40] A host is expected to make the stay in his home as pleasant as possible for his visitors and not to burden them with his troubles. Women are allowed to weep in dangerous situations, while young men would be ashamed of following their example. A clerk seen drunk in the street provokes disapproval, but a teacher in the same condition provokes moral indignation. When we are dividing goods with our friends we are expected to keep the less valuable share for ourselves, but this conduct would be rather surprising if it were the conduct of a master toward his servant. There are roles which last for all of life, like the role of a man or a woman; there are roles which last for years, like the professional roles; and there are roles which last for a few hours and may never be repeated, like the role of a bridegroom. In each case definite expectations are associated with the given role and definite duties are incumbent upon the person in that role: a son is expected to be griefstricken after the death of his mother. The fact that the stranger, in the novel of Albert Camus, spent the evening after the funeral of his mother in the cinema in the company of his lover, contributed to his being sentenced to death for killing a man without any obvious reason.

A person who wishes to promote mutual help among people should be aware of the fact that he cannot expect mutual help in a society where the role assignment is very rigid, as it is, for example, in the caste system of India, where people belonging to one caste cannot do the work allotted to another. There is an Indian tale which can be quoted as an illustration of this rigidity. A farmer had a dog and a donkey. One night, when both the dog and the donkey were asleep, a thief tried to enter the house. The dog did not notice, as he was soundly asleep, but the donkey heard the thief and made a great noise. The thief escaped and the farmer, awakening, learned what had happened. Then he beat the donkey for having assumed the duties of the dog.[41]

Relations within the Family and Their Influence

The greatest interest shown in the present day on the influence of family structure upon personality is in a large degree due to Freud. As everybody knows, it is to dramatic tensions in family life that Freud ascribes the development of the superego, which, assuming the functions of a censor, plays the role of conscience. From cultural anthropologists we learn about the innumerable varieties of family structure and emotional configuration between parents and children. In some cultures, the relations between husband and wife may be overtly intimate, while the relations of siblings, among the Trobriands, for example, are expected to be distant and blocked by different taboos. In other cultures the reverse holds true: a husband meets his wife in a clandestine way, while the relations of siblings are free from any control. In some cultures the relations between a father and his son are characterized by comradeship and familiarity. In others, a respectful distance is required from a son in relations with his father. The book *Authoritarian Personality*, published in 1950 (Theodor W. Adorno, *et al.*, New York), constitutes an important contribution to the study of this kind of problem. According to its authors, families with a father endowed with severe authority provide for the development of aggressive personalities, aggressive and at the same time full of reverence toward force and power, personalities looking for a scapegoat in order to express their frustration. According to Margaret Mead, children growing up in a climate of security do not exhibit a tendency toward competition and are more inclined to cooperation. A tendency toward competition is to be noticed where a person does not feel secure until he has persuaded himself of his unchallenged superiority.[42] Homosexuality has been attributed to having an overprotective mother, while Ruth Benedict, in speaking about Indians who at puberty assume the dress and occupations of women, sees in this a revolt against the role of male assigned to boys by their parents from their very early childhood.[43]

Because the family usually constitutes an economic unit, our attitude toward property depends in a large measure on the way goods in the family are owned and inherited. Among the Zuñi Indians the man, in this matrilineal society, works first for his mother and then for his wife's household. "The husbands of the daughters of the household have to return to their maternal households upon a domestic storm and will henceforth have no responsibility for feeding or housing their children which they leave behind." [44] In these conditions one cannot expect either a paternal feeling of responsibility for one's children or an attachment to property similar to that which we observe in the Euro-American world. Where the partition of goods follows rigid rules which take account of the place of the given individual in the local kinship system, we can hardly expect the existence of a notion of equalitarian justice.[45]

These are examples of possible effects of the family structure upon morality. To return once more to Freud and to the contemporary stress upon loving relations within the family, I should like to point out the fact that in the light of psychoanalytic theory children can develop a scrupulous conscience in a loving and tolerant family as well as in an authoritarian one. In the first case, because they fear the loss of their parents' love; in the second, because in the climate of strong prohibitions their tendency to aggression must be more intensely repressed and directed toward themselves, taking the form of pangs of conscience.

The family is treated among contemporary social psychologists and educators as a venerable institution whose functioning is of first importance for both the moral education and the happiness of people. It would be interesting to watch throughout the history of Euro-American civilization under what conditions the veneration given to the family increased and under what conditions it decreased. The family was not of great importance in the Greek

F

tradition. G. Glotz in his book *La Cité grecque* quotes and shares the complaints of Polybius that in his time people abstained altogether from marriage and, if they married, limited the number of their children to one or two.[46] According to the same Greek historian, at the end of the third century B.C., people bequeathed property to their friends for banqueting instead of leaving it to their relatives. Men had wives in order to have an heir to inherit their name, concubines to nurse them and attend them, and courtesans for pleasure. Hetaerae were thought of as more pleasant than wives because they had to do their best to keep the favors of men, while wives did not bother, since their union was secured by law. Hesiod in his *Works and Days* recommended that a family be limited to a single son. Both Plato and Aristotle were against having a large family.

Throughout most of European history, the family was not in great esteem among the aristocrats, although they were much interested in their noble lineage. The marriages of the nobility were purely conventional, adultery was often quite openly admitted, illegitimate sons could aspire to posts of high social standing. The importance attributed to fidelity and to a stable union was typical of the bourgeois ethos. Yet romanticism, which was of bourgeois origin, denounced the family for its philistinism and the attack was supported by Bohemian circles. Family life was also treated as an impediment to people serving a great cause. Saints did not hesitate to leave wives and children in order to pursue their own salvation in the desert. People devoted to the cause of social revolution used to free themselves of all family ties which they considered to be in conflict with their calling. A Polish writer of the beginning of the nineteen-twenties wrote in one of his books:

A family, like the one we know in our contemporary world, must be always a center of antisocial feelings. It plays the role of a cavern to which the rapacious man brings his booty. As long as a man lives mostly on what he has snatched from somebody else in one way or another, the family will not cease to constitute an emotional laboratory in which the most rapacious, egoistic, greedy and antisocial instincts will take a bucolic appearance, while the real substance will remain unchanged. Edward Christie

Banfield describes a poor Italian village.[47] He calls the attitude of its inhabitants "amoral familism." Each family has only the welfare of its kin in view and assumes that everybody else is doing the same.

Among well known criticisms of the family I must quote the opinions of George Bernard Shaw. In his introduction to *Getting Married* he considered the family as "an unnatural packing into little brick boxes of little parcels of humanity of ill assorted ages, with the old scolding and beating the young for behaving like young people, and the young hating and thwarting the old for behaving like old people." [48] The same attitude is voiced in Shaw's contention that the prohibition against incest is an expression of a natural repulsion, which everybody experiences toward his nearest relatives.

In connection with the difference of moral attitudes due to the amount of care given to children by their parents, I should like to mention a book by Florjan Znaniecki, published in 1934. This book was inspired by a commission, working under the chairmanship of W. F. Russell, Dean of Teacher's College in Columbia University in 1931. It was prepared at Columbia with the help of students and Znaniecki's colleagues and, so far as I know, was published only in Polish under the title *Contemporary Men and Future Civilization*. After an analysis of about seven hundred autobiographies and after studies of sixty educational institutions, Znaniecki and his collaborators distinguished three main groups of people characterized, among other things, by different moral attitudes. The first group was composed of men called "well-bred" by the author. The second, of people engaged in work for subsistence from their very early childhood. The third was composed of people dominated by the influence of play groups in which they participated. People who could not be included in any of these groups were called "deviants" by Znaniecki. The distinction of these three groups was not treated by the author as a classification. Since it was not a classification, there was no use to inquire about the principle on which it was based and to require its being exhaustive.

The three main groups characterized by Znaniecki were the groups he found in his empirical materials. People belonging to the so-called well-bred group have a long period of education under the constant solicitous supervision of their elders: home education, high school and college education. Their actions are constantly subjected to either praise or blame which orients them in their behavior. This fact makes them self-conscious, very sensitive to the opinions others have of them, very much interested in what Znaniecki calls their "reflected ego." These people manifest a tendency to self-perfection and, in order to be duly appreciated, seek the company of people who have a hierarchy of values similar to their own. Absorbed by their own excellence, they neglect civic virtues and are not capable of cooperation. Used to the friendly attitude of their mentors, they expect a similar attitude from strangers and are not prepared for a struggle for life, being convinced that their merits will be duly rewarded. In their moral judgments they take intention and sacrifice into account first of all, and are less interested in the effects of actions. Their morality is dominated by inhibitions. Well-bred people are convinced that the world is organized once and for all and that this organization is rational. They are conformist, not revolutionary, and in cases of great social changes are completely lost.

According to Znaniecki, a different kind of morality is developed by groups of people who were never the subject of great attention by their parents and were early engaged in their struggle for life. This morality is, in many respects, opposed to that of the well bred. Parents of this group have no time to guide the steps of their children by constant approval and disapproval. Consequently, there is no interest in oneself and in opinions of others concerning one's merits or demerits. One's person is rather unimportant. What matters is one's economic situation characterized not only by salary, but sometimes also by the degree of independence one has in the work. For people belonging to this group, economic forces dominate the world.

Well-bred people were familiar to Znaniecki through his personal experience and their description is vivid and convincing. The picture of people engaged early in economic activity is less persuasive and is blurred by the fact that this group is far from being homogeneous. Peasants as well as factory workers, artisans, small shopkeepers, and so on could be included in it. Still, the distinction of this group from that of well-bred people remains interesting.

The third group portrayed by Znaniecki is composed of people whose personalities were molded first of all by their playmates. A member of this group is used to cooperation and to having a definite function on the team. He observes rigorously the rules governing the game, although he is fully aware of their conventional character and knows that they can be changed at will with the agreement of the other players. The attitudes developed by boys and girls in these groups can find an expression in their later life in three areas: in social gatherings, in politics, and in war. Here a play spirit has an opportunity to develop. This play spirit is connected with an understanding that everybody has the right to play if he does not disturb others, that everybody has equal rights in the game if he observes accepted rules of fair play. The results of the activity are here less important, because play is always attractive for its own sake.

I will not dwell any longer upon Znaniecki's distinctions. This typology has been mentioned here because it brings to light some new factors which can shape moral attitudes. The third group reminds us of Piaget's distinction of different moral attitudes among children educated mostly under the pressure of adults and children spending most of their time under the influence of their playmates. But while Piaget stressed the importance of symmetrical relations, disregarding the fact that the members of these groups joined *for play*, the fact that they formed a playing group was considered particularly important, in Znaniecki's opinion, for the development of their morality.

The Way Moral Approval or Disapproval Depends on the Relation between Agent and Partner

When I was discussing the supposedly beneficial consequences of the division of labor, I mentioned a rather critical opinion referring to the fact that the growing specialization of professions tends to make human relations impersonal. By impersonal I meant a relation similar to that between a customer and a clerk in a post office or between a passenger in a taxi and the taxi driver. In both cases we are not interested in the clerk and the taxi driver as individuals. One clerk could just as well be replaced by any other clerk and either of them could be replaced by an automaton. The situation is different in personal relations where the fact that we have to do with one person and not with another is relevant.

I have recalled this distinction because actions praised or blamed in personal relations are sometimes neither praised nor blamed in impersonal relations. Let us take egoism as an example. We consider a man an egoist when, in a case of conflict of interests, he tends to favor his own. The emotional content of the word "egoist" is pejorative and so the word is not applied in a situation when we have our own interests in view, and when our relation to our partner is impersonal. In a simple commercial transaction from hand to hand, the seller wishes to gain as much as possible and the buyer to pay as little as possible. We have here a conflict of interests but neither of the partners expects a sacrifice from the other side. The relation is impersonal and the preference given to our own interests is not to be taken as egoistic. In personal relations our obligations are different. It is not pleasant to bargain with a friend. Some historians of trade are of the opinion that the institution of a middleman, a mediator, was invented in order to depersonalize commercial transactions and to make easier an attitude of exploitation, embarrassing in face to face relations.

The kind of relations between people also affects our notion of altruism. Parents who prepare Christmas gifts for their children, even if they do it with some personal sacrifice, are not called altruists, although the definition of altruism may be fulfilled by their conduct itself. While we have frequent opportunities to be altruists in impersonal relations or in relations personal but hostile, it is easiest to be an egoist in personal and friendly relations. In a deadly fight nobody expects a kind regard for one's opponent. We are not termed egoists when we defend our life against attack, although we sacrifice the good of our opponent for our own. This sacrifice of the good of our opponent is also fully admitted in games. Whoever plays chess, having constantly in view not his own but the opposite side's interests, behaves in an intolerable way, as the game makes sense and is enjoyed only when there is a conflict of interests and each player is working for his own victory, taking advantage of all his adversary's weaknesses. It is in the interests of both players to be as ruthless as possible because this attitude is essential for the enjoyment which the game is expected to provide.

Long ago people noticed that the rules of fair play in love relations between the sexes differ from the rules in other social and business relations. To deceive, to tempt, to entitle to hope without any intention of fulfilling expectations—these have been common practices among men and women honest and reliable on other occasions.[49] English novelists of the eighteenth century opposed this duality. The promise of marriage in seducing a girl was, according to Henry Fielding, as sacred as any promise should be.

Personality Factors in Morality

How far strictly personal factors and, first of all, emotional make-up, can influence moral opinions is the subject of a recent empirical study by two American authors, J. Retting and B. Pasamanick. They asked 489 American and 513 Korean students a number of questions concerning moral problems. The results of this inquiry have been published in the periodical *Sociometry*.[50] The answers given proved that the difference of moral opinions (with the exception of a group of norms, which were concerned with conduct conventionally but not intrinsically wrong) was greater *within* the ethnic groups than between the two ethnic groups investigated. This suggests a hypothesis that these differences were due to personality traits—an interesting result, which, however, needs further verification.

The Role of Individuals in the Development of Moral Opinions

The role of individuals in the development of morality has been, as a rule, underestimated by Marxists in their tendency to stress first of all the importance of class struggle and class determinants. In spite of this opinion, one may, I think, with some degree of probability, attribute an influence on moral opinions to Charles

Dickens whose picture of the inhumanity of the poor law (*Oliver Twist*) or the atrocities of the debtors' prisons moved the public opinion of England. It would also be possible to contend that Victorian morality could not remain unchanged after Geroge Bernard Shaw's plays. Some people consider that A. J. Cronin's novel *The Citadel* contributed to the reform of medical service in England, a reform based on the moral conviction that human suffering cannot be the object of gain. It would be difficult to prove that both Cronin and Albert Schweitzer, with his postulate of respect of human life, were only mouthpieces of their class interests.

The Role of the Past

There are some traits in societies which one cannot explain without reference to their past. Thus the stress in America on being a good neighbor and on mutual help has often been attributed to the pioneer period. The same stress is laid on mutual help in Australia for the same reason.

In Poland one can notice a particular repugnance connected with informing. Hundreds of years of foreign rule, years of German occupation, have contributed to developing an attitude of solidarity against those in power. To break this solidarity by communicating to authorities a transgression of the law encounters reluctance, even if one is persuaded that the wrong done ought to be punished.

Knowledge and Morality

To my previous considerations I must still add some remarks concerning the mutual influence of knowledge at the disposal of the group and its morality, of art and morality, religion and morality, law and morality.

Examples of the influence of our beliefs concerning reality are easy to quote and there exist authors who contend that all differences of moral opinion are due to differences in belief. Some primitive communities judge it necessary to kill the mother of twins and the twins, as two children must have two fathers and are an ocular demonstration of adultery. In Europe, as late as the eighteenth century, people were allowed to tease for twopence insane persons chained to a wall. This practice, unthinkable today, was related to the fact that the insane were thought to be possessed by the devil. The Zuñi Indians are not allowed to show or feel anger or any ill feeling during ceremonies aimed at bringing rain, as they believe the ceremonies would not be successful. The Hopi Indians disapprove of unfriendly attitudes toward people because you can never know when you have to do with a sorcerer, whose revenge could prove dangerous. The Hopi rear their children without punishing them because they believe that there exists an immanent justice which will reward the good and punish the wrongdoer without any intervention on their part. Everybody knows in what large measure our opinions about human nature influence the content of moral precepts. The number of prohibitions must grow if human nature is believed to be principally wicked. The psychoanalytic opinion that human beings are torn by internal conflicts has contributed to a high estimation of the value of integration, adjustment, and harmony.

It is impossible to omit here mention of a book which tries to show to what degree a definite doctrine has affected the morality of the United States. I have in mind the book of La Piere, already cited, entitled *The Freudian Ethic: An Analysis of the Subversion of the American Character*. The popularity of psychoanalysis in the United States is, in the author's opinion, striking. According to the ethic called Protestant (an ethic not necessarily connected with Protestantism and giving an ideal of character rather than a code of morality), the ideal man was self-reliant and independent, a man of action, full of enterprise, a man responsible for his own welfare. The God of Protestants was a demanding God. He was a God of achievement through adversity. He required men to sacrifice current satisfactions to future ones. For the Protestant ethic not the consumption of wealth but its accumulation was important. People who adopted this creed were self-confident. They believed in progress. They believed in reason. The man who submitted passively to hardships was, for them, an unworthy creature.

The picture of man in psychoanalysis was quite different.

Freudian doctrine in La Piere's opinion is "a doctrine of social irresponsibility and personal despair." [51] The man is here the victim of social circumstances and he is antagonistic toward society. Conflict between the individual and society is regarded as inevitable. The terminology of people who subscribe to psychoanalysis is worth attention. "In their discourse," writes La Piere, "there is recurrent reference to guilt feelings, personal insecurity, unconstructed personality, instability, . . . frustration, aggressive tendencies, trauma, and the all-inclusive term 'tensions.'" What the Freudians hold as ideal is a precarious balance between id, ego, and superego. In their doctrine there is a complete absence of any sense of obligation toward others.[52]

As a result of these opinions the home as well as the school indulge in being permissive. They give without requiring anything. The child has first of all to be well adjusted and in order to make him well adjusted he has to be protected from frustration. Passive conformity is the result. Fortunately, according to the author, the Freudian ethic has not been adopted by the workers. It is a doctrine of the new bourgeoisie.

I have quoted this book at some length as an example of the influence attributed to a psychological theory in shaping the morality of a continent. Examples of how scientific theories and discoveries provoke moral change can easily be multiplied. I consider as particularly important changes brought about by technology. The invention of gunpowder contributed to the decline of chivalry, a topic to which I shall return. The development of contraceptives has brought about great changes in sexual morality. Now problems arise in the medical profession with the possibility of affecting irreversible changes in human character by chemical treatment. Are doctors entitled to change the personality of people? New moral problems have arisen in connection with the invention of atomic weapons. Nowadays people travel much more and much faster than they did before, which makes for better understanding. Our growing sociological knowledge also helps this understanding in many ways, for example, by freeing us from the intervention of stereotypes, which by their fixity raise a barrier between people of different nations. Thomas Burton Bottomore is of the opinion that sociological training, by disclosing some of the external factors influencing conduct, has diminished the scope of moral praise and blame.[53] The development of empirical research in the field of the sociology of law has put into doubt the efficacy of the death penalty as a deterrent, and the efficacy of a severe penal code for preventing crime.

Our contemporary social psychology has produced several studies concerning factors influencing tolerance, among them the part played in it by our growing knowledge, our enlarged education. There is an a priori assumption of a positive correlation between education and tolerance. In fact, the situation proves to be complicated because we ought always to ask, "tolerance for what?" Women reputed to be less tolerant than men proved more permissive than men when offences against property were concerned and less lenient when they were asked about offences against morality. Growing knowledge seems to make men more severe, an attitude attributed to a new awareness of the serious threat crime presents to society or to an increasing identification with judicial authority.[54]

Some cultural anthropologists think that the so-called world view (*Weltanschauung*) is very important, if not decisive, for moral opinions. Thus, for example, Ethel M. Albert, in her paper "On Classification of Values," recommends beginning with the general view of life of primitive people in order to study their moral opinions. The author supports her statement by referring to the Navajo Indians.[55]

I do not think that there exists any necessary connection between the world view and moral opinions. The moral opinions of Bishop Berkeley do not seem to have been suggested by his conviction that material objects exist only through being perceived. Utilitarianism in England was professed in different combinations. It was supported by the English deists like Thomas Chubb and by William Paley, a representative of the Anglican church. Utilitarians also differed widely in their political opinions. For Charles Darwin, a struggle for existence, which he observed all around him, was the basic factor stimulating progress. For Kropotkin, the Russian anarchist, it was mutual help, observed all around, among men as well as among animals. These two opposite world views were accompanied in these two authors by striking similarities in their moral opinions.

It is possible to quote instances where the relation is rather the reverse and where moral opinions determine general statements concerning the world. According to some people, the belief in a unity reigning among all living beings, and in the interconnection of all that happens in the universe, was adopted in order to prove that, whenever we do some good to ourselves, others profit from it. The same creed could be used not to support egoism, but to promote altruism, in showing that whenever we wrong others we also wrong ourselves. The belief of the ancient Stoics which formed a part of their world view, namely that causal chains of what is good and what is wrong never cross, was due to a moral repulsion at the idea that good actions can have bad effects and wrong actions good consequences. Many people were shocked by the theory of Mandeville in his *Fable of the Bees* that good and evil actions were causally interrelated. It would be possible to argue that the inexorable laws which, according to Marx, have dominated history were suggested by his moral aspirations. The need of brotherhood and the conviction that it was to be found among proletarians suggested the idea that history was moving in the direction of their victory. Karl Popper in his *Open Society* is very convincing in showing the moral background of Marx's theories.

Art and Morality

The relation of art and morality has been rarely neutral in the eyes of theorists. While some authors have recommended the cultivation of art, or at least, of an interest in artistic creativeness as the best way to reach a moral standard worthy of approval, others have considered art as dangerous for morality. Plato, although he adhered to the Greek ideal of the *kalokagathia*, the ideal of a union of goodness and beauty, expelled poets from his ideal state because they contributed to the corruption of society. Plato as well as Aristotle considered music particularly important for moral education. He was quite definite about the kind of music which could be admitted in his ideal state and the kind which must be prohibited. Because of its great moral influence, art had to be submitted to strict state control. Tragedy was expected to edify people. Plays must represent vice punished and virtue duly rewarded. Any novelty in music was, according to Plato, dangerous, because a change in its style always had repercussions in politics. Aristotle was known for his theory of catharsis or purification, attributed to the influence of art. His commentators have not been unanimous in their interpretation of this purifying influence. Some of them have seen in it a *sublimation* of emotions, while others have seen rather a *liberation* from emotions, the second opinion being, so far as I know, dominant.

In spite of some restrictions, the Greek tradition agreed not only in the possibility of integrating more goodness and beauty, but in considering this unity indispensable. The Greek historian Polybius (ca. 208–126 B.C.), tells us that the inhabitants of Arcadia, his native country, thought that music was absolutely indispensable to those who were not to be considered barbarians. They could confess without a blush any other incompetence, but the admission of not being able to sing was shameful to them.[56]

Modern times present a great variety of opinions concerning the relation of art and morality. Lord Shaftesbury in England at the beginning of the eighteenth century united goodness and beauty in his conception of a model man, whom he called Virtuoso. Moral sense was for him very close to taste. This opinion is typical of the aristocracy and we shall return to it later on. Rousseau denounced the demoralizing effects of art and this view was later upheld by Tolstoy. He argued that the more we devote ourselves to art the greater is our distance from morality. Romanticism admitted a close connection between art and morality as well in the artist as in his audience. Shelley stressed the importance of the development of imagination both for art and for morality and the close relation of our sensitiveness to beauty and to moral worth.

The relation of art and morality absorbed Thomas Mann very much. He thought that there is an incompatibility between being an artist and being an honest man, at least in the bourgeois conception of honesty. Adrian Leverkühn, the hero of his fascinating novel, *Doctor Faustus*, owes his musical genius to a pact with the devil.

Among sociologists who have discussed this relationship, Emil Durkheim was the one who saw a conflict between art and morality. A great development of artistic activity in a society was, in his opinion, a symptom of imminent danger. This danger was due to the incompatibility of attitudes needed in art and attitudes required for morality. Art revolts against any constraint, while morality needs discipline. Art needs a free expression, while morality needs obedience to authority.

Among psychologists I must mention here the role attributed to art by Freud. According to him, art plays a double role in morality. In artistic activity we can search for a sublimation of our instincts—the notion of sublimation being a laudatory notion implying a realization of what is morally desirable. Art for the artist and for his audience could, in addition, offer an occasion for what is called *Ersatzbefriedigung*, that is, a substitutive satisfaction of our needs, whose direct satisfaction could be detrimental to the life of the society.

Morality and Religion

The relations between morality and knowledge, morality and art, morality and religion suggest groups of problems so vast that I can only point to some of them. In these relations moral phenomena are, first, treated as dependent variables. A discussion of morality as dependent on or as independent of religion ought to begin with the question of what kind of dependence we can have in mind.

1. This dependence may be a question of origin. Many people believe that our moral code has been given to man by supernatural beings, who play not only the role of lawgivers, but also, after our death, the role of judges of our merits and our sins or transgressions against divine law. David Bidney calls religions which attribute a moral role to their gods, moralistic religions. According to him, such religions are in the minority, since most religious creeds imagine their gods as absolutely indifferent in matters of morality.[57] Durkheim considered that the mystical im-

perativeness of moral commandments is due to the fact that morality was originally related to religion. It would be interesting to verify this hypothesis and to see whether the imperative character of moral commandments is also to be found in cultures which, in Bidney's terminology, are not moralistic.

The problem of whether we owe to God our moral code was a major one in the eighteenth century. Shaftesbury pointed to the fact that in order to trust Revelation we must be persuaded that God is good and does not deceive us, and this presupposes a need for moral values preceding Revelation. The deists' belief in a natural morality, a creed very popular in the eighteenth century, was at the same time a belief in a morality independent in its origin of any deity, because it was a morality common to countries differing in their religious dogmas.

2. The second interpretation of the opinion that morality depends on religion suggests a *logical* dependence of moral valuations and precepts on one side, and religious dogmas on the other. Thus disapproval of divorce has been supported by referring to the dogma that a union made before God can be dissolved only by Him. The disapproval of homosexuality was connected with the religious assumption that only sexual relations which led to procreation were admissible. Similarly one can defend indifference toward man's cruelty to animals by referring to the assumption that animals have been created to serve man or to the assumption that animals have no souls. Suicide has been condemned for many reasons. Among them was the argument that only God could dispose of our lives as it was He who created us. The same argument was applied in discussions concerning euthanasia. Abortion was condemned because the embryo was believed to be endowed from the very beginning with an immortal soul. Disapproval of nakedness was connected with the opinion concerning the sinfulness of sex.

3. In all these examples certain moral rules are logically dependent on some religious creed. However, we can speak of dependence also when there is no direct logical relation but when one can see the influence of religion on the content of some moral convictions. The importance attributed to sexual ethic, which can be illustrated by the fact that in many languages the word "moral-

ity" is restricted to this area, was certainly due to the influence of religion. The necessity of sanctifying sexual intercourse by marriage was also influenced by religion. "The woman who breaks the taboo uncovered by the ceremony, is stamped once for all with the scarlet letter, without regard to the question whether she was an experienced temptress or one whose fault was merely to have loved and trusted too much." [58] She is condemned once for all, she is treated like a piece of damaged goods in the social market.

4. The last kind of dependence of morality on religion is the dependence of our behavior upon our creed. The question, whether morality depends on religion in this sense amounts to the question, whether a man can be honest without being religious. The question is purely empirical. Ethical writers of the eighteenth century were convinced that it was possible and pointed to the Chinese who were held in high esteem at that time, although they were not Christians and although Confucianism did not teach the existence of supernatural beings. To what degree religious motives induce people to do what is considered right and restrain them from what is considered wrong should be the subject of empirical research. In what measure are people restrained from stealing by the idea that they have a witness in a supernatural being and in what measure are they restrained by fear of being caught and punished or by sympathy with the man they plan to rob?

Because some religions have a moral content, those which were termed by Bidney *moralistic*, the impact of religion on morality often proves to be the impact of one morality upon another. The impact of religion on politics, economics, and family life has been recently empirically investigated by G. Lenski in a sample of 750 Detroiters. Lenski was concerned with questions like the impact of religion on attitudes toward gambling, drinking, birth control, divorce. He arrived at a general formula which he called the principle of social hedonism, which runs as follows. "When two established and institutionalized religious groups support opposing moral norms, the less demanding norm tends to win the less committed members of *both* groups." In times of crisis and in newly formed sects, rigorous moral norms may be established and the enthusiasm generated may for a certain time overcome the "normal" attraction of hedonism.[59]

Morality and Law

This also is a vast subject which I can treat only very briefly, leaving aside for the present moment the question of the concept of law as related to the concept of morality, a problem which I have discussed in a separate paper.[60] By law I shall mean here the content of penal and civil codes. Nobody contests the fact that penal law is imbued with moral elements. Some moral prohibitions are repated almost word for word in penal codes, for example, "do not kill," "do not steal." Our civil codes are in a similar situation. In a book entitled *La règle morale dans les obligations civiles*, G. Ripert tries to show that "law in its most technical part is dominated by moral commands" ("Le droit dans sa partie la plus technique est dominé par la loi morale).[61] Moral elements are to be found in the content of laws and also in the motivation of lawgivers. They have a definite hierarchy of values, although this is not explicitly shown. The priority of monogamy over other possible forms of marriage, the value of stability in family life, the necessity of avoiding conflicts which are considered a social evil, the tendency to defend the interests of the weak, such as the interests of children in cases of divorce—these are values which lawgivers wish to defend. Moral elements are not only present in the very content of laws and the ends which lawgivers have in view. They are also to be found in the administration of law, in legal procedure. Some persons are allowed to refuse to give testimony on moral grounds. The notion of natural law has a purely moral character. It was referred to in the Nuremburg trial in the absence of laws which would permit the sentencing of people for mass murder.

The influence of morality on law is much more conspicuous than the influence of law on morality. Although William Graham Sumner in his *Folkways*[62] argued that legislation cannot make mores, yet the educative function of law is not to be disregarded. The very excess of legal enactments can have undesirable moral effects, as the Roman historian Tacitus pointed out. Unrealistic prohibitions, which cannot for purely technical reasons be respected, teach people to transgress the law. The question whether

G

a severe or a lenient law contributes in a higher degree to the repression of delinquency is, as everybody knows, a subject of very lively discussion in capitalist as well as in socialist countries. The demoralizing effects of penitentiaries have been denounced by many contemporary writers on the basis of empirical investigations. Law is conservative, but the idea of the necessity of a radical change in our endeavors to rehabilitate criminals is pervading most contemporary writings on this subject.

Moral Phenomena as Independent Variables

According to the title of these lectures, I planned to review different determinants of moral attitudes and of moral rules supported by these attitudes. So far I have been concerned with a one-sided dependence, although it is quite evident that the factors influencing morality are in most cases influenced in turn by it. This interdependence is especially striking in the last examples I discussed. Art, religion, and law reflect the morality of a given society. Moral aspirations of people are expressed in their notion of the deity, whose excellence is conceived differently according to the moral convictions of the believers.

Before I return to social determinants of morality in order to discuss in a more detailed way the influence of class distinctions, I would like to mention here some widely discussed theories concerning the role of moral ideas in economics.

Max Weber's well-known theory treated the Protestant ethic as a codeterminant in promoting the development of early capitalism. Although this theory is widely known, I should like to recall here some of its main points. In reconstructing Weber's arguments it seems advisable to begin with the following factual statements: 1) Weber noticed that in his country the biggest factories were in the hands of Protestants and more particularly in the hands of Calvinists. 2) He also noted that the income tax paid by the latter amounted to much greater sums than the income tax paid by Catholics. 3) He attracted attention to the fact that Catholic countries, like Italy and Spain, were not industrialized, while in Protestant ones the process of industrialization was in full development. 4) He pointed out that in Germany, Catholics were more numerous in colleges giving a classic humanistic education than in colleges giving technical training.

These facts suggested that there was something in Protestantism which fostered economic activity and the accumulation of wealth. Weber believed that among the factors, were the Puritan ethic and the Calvinist dogma of predestination.[63] Calvin believed people to be blessed or damned by God in advance. Worldly success was an outward sign of inward grace. This success could be attained only by hard work, frugality, and renunciation, by an ascetic life which Weber called worldly asceticism (*Innerweltliche Askese*) in opposition to the asceticism practiced by the saints in the Middle Ages. This attitude resulted in an accumulation of wealth and was one of the factors contributing to the development of a spirit of capitalism and of capitalism itself. A tendency to acquire wealth was by no means unknown in different countries and times, but what Weber considered new was that the acquisition of wealth was now being treated as a calling and had turned into a mass phenomenon.

A distinction must be made between the statement that the Puritan ethic gave rise to the spirit of capitalism and the statement that it led to capitalism. The first is a psychological statement about the correlation of two psychological facts, while the second is an assertion about the connection between a moral attitude which is a psychological fact, and the development of capitalism, which is an objective fact.

Both these statements were treated by Weber as something more than historical statements. He had a tendency to generalize these statements and to support a general hypothesis which could be formulated as follows: whenever a given society develops virtues like thrift, frugality, renunciation, one can expect an accumulation of wealth, stimulating constant new investments. In this general form Weber's theory was criticized by people who tried to show that Calvinism adopted by aristocracy (as happened in Poland) had different results. These critics wished to show that *who* accepts Calvinism and *under what conditions* are facts which cannot be disregarded.

While Weber's psychological statement is doubtful, his historical thesis about the correlation of the development of capitalism and the practice of Puritan virtues is much more convincing. In the first, it is not clear why Puritan virtues are expected to foster the spirit of capitalism and especially why the dogma of predestination should play an important role in it. Why should the dogma of presdestination make us believe that we belong to the blessed by our success in making money? It would be equally possible to conclude that we are blessed from the fact of our survival *in spite of complete idleness.* According to the Greeks, a belief in predestination does not stimulate activity, but contributes to idleness (*logòs argòs*). Edward Westermarck in his book *Christianity and Morals* [64] rightly points out that only in certain social conditions could one hit upon the idea of wealth as criterion of belonging to the chosen.

The dogma of presdestination is certainly very useful for justifying one's own privileges and for quieting the conscience. But its role in fostering the spirit of capitalism, best expressed according to Weber in Franklin's slogan, "Time is money," is rather dubious. Sects like the Quakers and the Mormons, which did not accept predestination, also proved very successful in acquiring wealth. The fact that the Quakers, refusing to take the required oath, were excluded in England from many offices, forced them into economic activity.

As a second example of the influence of morality on economics I should like to mention the popular distinction between guilt cultures and shame cultures.

In her book *The Chrysanthemum and the Sword,* Ruth Benedict writes as follows:

> In anthropological studies of different cultures the distinction of those which rely heavily on shame and those that rely heavily on guilt is an important one. A society that inculcates absolute standards of morality and relies on men's developing a conscience is a guilt culture by definition, but a man in such a society may, as in the United States, suffer in addition from shame when he accuses himself of gaucheries which are in no way sins. He may be exceedingly chagrined about not dressing appropriately for the occasion or about a slip of the tongue. In a culture where shame is a major sanction, people are chagrined about acts which we expect people to feel guilty about. This chagrin can be very

intense and it cannot be relieved, as guilt can be, by confession and atonement.[65]

According to this author, true *shame* cultures rely on external sanctions for good behavior, as shame is a reaction to other people's criticism. True guilt cultures rely on an internalized conviction of sin. American culture is a culture of guilt, while the culture of Japan is a culture of shame.

The importance of the feeling of guilt for the development of culture as a whole was stressed by Freud. In Chapter VIII of his work *Das Unbehagen in der Kultur* (*Civilization and Its Discontents*) Freud tried to show that a feeling of guilt was especially important for the development of culture and that men have had to pay for progress with a loss of happiness due to the increase in the feeling of guilt. This increase must be connected with the fact that more advanced cultures require of people that they more fully master their tendency to aggression. This aggression, having no outlet, becomes internalized and is expressed in guilt feelings.

Margaret Mead also distinguishes between cultures of guilt and cultures of shame in her introduction to the book *Cooperation and Competition among Primitive Peoples*.[66] This distinction has been criticized. One critic, M. Singer, contests the distinction itself and the theory that the feeling of guilt is dynamic and leads to an intensification of economic life.[67] The distinction of cultures of shame and cultures of guilt on the basis of two types of sanctions is, in Singer's view, unsatisfactory because shame can be internalized (a situation admitted by Margaret Mead) and is thus hard to distinguish from guilt. Singer expresses some doubts about its application in the studies of Kluckhohn and Leighton concerning white children in the United States and the children of Navajo Indians. In these studies the white children, who were brought up by the aid of an internalized ideal of personality, were reputed to be guided by a feeling of guilt, while Navajo children, who accepted standards as part of the external environment to which an adjustment must be made, were motivated by a feeling of shame.

Singer points out the need for replying to three questions: 1) by what general criteria may we distinguish a shame culture from a guilt culture? 2) What kind of psychological data will furnish evidence for the prevalence of shame or guilt in a culture? 3) To what extent may we interpret characteristic anxieties and emotional emphases of a culture as "projections" of unconscious guilt? [68]

Clyde Kluckhohn and Dorothea Leighton admit that cultures of shame are less progressive than cultures of guilt.[69] In reply, Singer recalls the fact that three major pathologies of modern civilization—war, dictatorship, and mental disease—have often been attributed to a "heightened sense of guilt." Progress, in his opinion, does not depend on repression and the increase of an unconscious sense of guilt, but is associated with the delimitation and specialization of the sense of moral responsibility. Psychoanalysts derive the sense of guilt from repressed hostility and a repressed tendency to aggression. But, as we read in the same book, the assumption that aggression must be repressed in all cultures is not admissible.

The critical remarks cited above seem to be convincing and I should like to add to them. While authors, like Margaret Mead, have been inclined to treat cultures of guilt as rather rare, admitting that the great majority of primitive cultures have been cultures of shame, other writers profess opposite views. The well-known German author, H. Kelsen, is of the opinion that thinking in terms of guilt and punishment is typical of primitive societies. Kelsen quotes as an example a myth, very popular in Europe as well as Asia, explaining why fishes are mute. According to this myth, fishes were told of Noah's Flood before it occurred but were ordered to keep the information secret. Because they spread the news, they were punished by eternal muteness.[70] Another German writer, E. Topitsch, cites a number of instances where different physical phenomena have been explained in terms of guilt and punishment by primitive people.[71] It has often been pointed out that every calamity and every failure, whether it be prolonged drought, illness, death, or unsuccessful hunting, is usually ascribed by primitives to wrongdoing. According to Redfield, primitive man feels himself tied to his group so much, that he has an opportunity to be worried by guilt more often than we do.

Why should a feeling of guilt be expected to lead to intense activity? A probable answer is that a man, motivated by a feeling of guilt, constantly tries to prove his worth by his achievements. I agree that a feeling of guilt may sometimes be a factor contributing to heightened economic activity, but I do not regard it as a necessary condition. I doubt whether the intense industrialization and economic activity of different contemporary countries can be attributed to a feeling of guilt, and to the promotion of a Protestant personality type, which Margaret Mead attributes to the Soviet Union.

The feeling of guilt was referred to as an example of a moral factor influencing economic life. We can find remarks on the same topic in many writers. The prosperity of a nation has usually been ascribed to personal virtues, a spirit of enterprise, thrift, diligence, and all the virtues recommended by the so-called Protestant ethic. In *The Fable of the Bees*, Bernard Mandeville, who liked paradoxes, tried to prove the contrary, that not virtues but vices are necessary for prosperity:

> "Fools only strive
> To make a great and honest hive. . . .
> Without great vices, is a vain
> Utopia seated in the brain.
> Envy itself and Vanity
> Were Ministers of Industry.
> Fraud, Luxury and Pride must live,
> While we the benefits receive."

The Fable of the Bees is a demonstration of the paradox that private vices contribute to public benefits, if by benefits we understand general prosperity and political prestige. It is interesting to note that Engels in his book on Feuerbach wrote: "It is precisely the wicked passions of man—greed and lust of power—which since the emergence of class antagonisms serve as the levers of historical development." [72]

Methodological Remarks

The examples of determinants, which I reviewed in my previous considerations, are far from exhaustive, but are now sufficiently numerous to allow some methodological remarks. The first one is connected with different possible interpretations of the word "influence."

He who speaks about the influence of climate on morality refers to instances like the fact that people grow lazy when the heat is excessive or that they adopt in hot countries a hierarchy of values in which nonactivity is particularly praised, for instance, the ideal of nirvana. When, in turn, one speaks of the proportion of men and women as influencing morality one does not refer to influence on the character of the people involved or on their value orientation. In this case people must resort to new means of securing the same values, as happens in societies which adopt polyandry because women are scarce. The satisfaction of sexual needs is here treated as a value as much as it is in societies which practice polygyny, but a different proportion of sexes suggests different methods of securing the same values.

When we speak about the density of population as influencing morals, we have again to do with a new situation which provokes conflicts, unknown in societies where population is sparse, and thus requires new rules for their solution. New conditions are also created in the case of the division of labor. Its influence consists in making people aware of their mutual dependence and of the advantages of solidarity. When one speaks of professional ethics one admits that professions can influence morality. One can also have in mind then, the fact that a profession may mold the character of the man engaged in it and, consequently, change those aspects of his behavior to which some moral rules refer.

A profession may also put men into situations which force them to formulate new prescriptions sometimes contradictory to those accepted outside the profession or which emphasize certain duties not considered important by the society as a whole.

The influence of class distinctions on morality is still more complicated and many-sided and it will be analyzed in a separate chapter.

Up to now I have simply enumerated the factors which influence morality. He who would like to verify these hypotheses would have to resort to comparative studies. Such studies encounter many difficulties, especially in the comparison of very different cultures. What must be considered as belonging to morality in a primitive society with a frame of concepts quite different from our own? In studying its morality we can observe how people of the given society react to behavior which in our own society is either praised or blamed. Westermarck did this when he asked how people of different primitive societies evaluate killing, lying, cheating, premarital sexual experience, divorce, and so on. But by adopting this method we use concepts elaborated in our own culture and risk missing important approvals or disapprovals not fitting our conceptual scheme.

The other possible method takes psychology as the point of departure. The investigator may in this case begin with some typical reaction, for example, the reaction called moral indignation, and observe which actions provoke this reaction in a given society. Such a method was adopted by Richard Brandt in his analysis of Hopi ethic. But it is not easy to decide whether one has to do in a given case with truly disinterested moral indignation or with the indignation which is felt when we find ourselves robbed, an indignation which William McDougall refused to call moral as it is not disinterested.

In surveys and polls done in contemporary societies, the sociologist is much concerned with whether his sample is representative of the population he studies. In the study of a primitive society the researcher often generalizes answers given by individual respondents as if there were unanimity among all the members, an assumption which is not at all convincing.

The verification or rather falsification of a hypothesis concerning a determinant of morality is easier when the determinant is considered decisive. If we interpret Montesquieu as someone who treats climate as decisive, following his statement that "the empire of the climate is the first, the most powerful, of all empires," we may falsify this claim by showing, either that the morality of two societies living in different climates are analogous, or that societies living in the same climate differ esentially in their moral opinions. Thus some authors point out that the Chukchi and the Eskimos, although inhabiting the same difficult Arctic environment, possess different social, political, and religious institutions, and the same is true of the Pueblo and the Navajo Indians living in analogous desert areas. The Chukchi of Siberia develop in their environment an accumulative spirit manifested in hoarding beyond any realistic need, while the Eskimos have no impetus to accumulate.

The economic factor, certainly very important, but sometimes overestimated, is not decisive for the development of morality since we can point to analogous moral phenomena in capitalist and socialist countries, in spite of their different economic structure. The growth of juvenile delinquency which constitutes an important social problem nowadays may be cited as an example. The description of American gangs given by American authors also applies very well to Polish hoodlums. I mention this fact because in one of our Polish studies of hoodlum groups, the author tried to explain these phenomena by the great social changes brought about by the transition from capitalism to socialism. While the old morality was in many points no longer binding in the new system, the new morality was supposed to have had insufficient time to take root. This supposedly caused disoriented youth to adhere to delinquent groups. This explanation does not seem satisfactory because in a socialist country like Czechoslovakia the problem scarcely exists, while in capitalist countries like Sweden, Great Britain, and the United States it causes much trouble to educators as well as to the police.

If the factor supposed to influence our moral life is not taken as decisive but as a co-determinant of morality, the falsification of the hypothesis is of course much more difficult. The situation does not differ here from the situation of any hypothesis concerning causal relations in social life, where the number of variables is so great and they are so closely interrelated that we are never sure of having excluded the interference of unexpected factors or those which, although taken into account, are supposed to be unimportant in the given case.

I should like to close these remarks by calling attention to the fact that the arguments which we had occasion to cite were often elliptical in that they assumed general psychological statements taken for granted. Thus, when we are told that growing density of population requires new rules, the assumption is made that people want to avoid conflicts. When we are told that the principle of reciprocity stressed by Malinowski can work only in small groups

with face to face relations, it is assumed that only in these conditions is the motivation *"do ut des"* possible. When we argue that
where there is a great density of population life is cheap, we tacitly
assume that people do not respect things which are plentiful and
which can be easily replaced. These plausible guesses, as Svend
Ranulf would call them,[73] may sometimes raise doubts.

In order to show how difficult the explanation of moral
phenomena can be, I should like to render an account of discussions concerning two moral facts; the growing freedom of sexual
relations and the growth of juvenile delinquency.

The Kinsey report on sexual behavior was initiated in 1938
and completed over the course of fifteen years. In the foreword to
the volume on the sexual behavior of the human female we read
the following:

> In the United States the twentieth century has been a period
> of exceedingly rapid and revolutionary change in sex attitudes and
> practices. Whereas throughout the nineteenth century the puri-
> tanic attitude in sexual matters was dominant in the United
> States, since the turn of the century both mores and practices
> have been in flux. What fifty years ago could not have been
> mentioned in a social group—sexual and reproductive happen-
> ings and experiences—now are spoken of without inhibitions.
> These changes are in part a product of 1) woman's progressive
> sexual and economic emancipation; 2) the all-pervasive influence
> of Freud's views and discoveries; and 3) the exposure during the
> World Wars of millions of American youth to cultures and
> peoples whose sex codes and practices differ greatly from those in
> which they had been reared.[74]

In an article called "The Sexual Revolution," Pearl S. Buck
gives several examples of this change.[75] According to her, not only
young but even older women are allowing themselves a sexual
freedom which in the prewar period would have horrified not only
their mothers but themselves. In the past men demanded chastity
in their wives and virginity in their brides. Now "it does not seem
to matter to most men, whether they marry virgins or not."

This revolution is confined neither to America nor to capitalist countries. Books prohibited in England, like *Lady Chatterley's
Lover*, now have the *nihil obstat*. H. Havelock Ellis (1859–1939)
suffered severe censure and legal restrictions a few decades earlier

when he wanted to publish his scholarly findings concerning sexual life in England.[76] This censure would be unthinkable today. The House of Commons voted recently to repeal all penalties for homosexual acts committed in private by consenting adults.

In Poland full recognition of children born outside marriage is realized not only legally but also socially. Divorces in cases of a consensus on both sides and in the absence of children are easily obtained; abortion in certain circumstances is easy too.

Several causes were suggested for these rapid and important changes, which deserve the name of revolution. "The effects of two world wars have changed both men and women," writes Pearl Buck. "Men living for long periods abroad in an atmosphere of imminent death, away from home ties and restraint seem no longer to demand chastity in women." They have been used to swift satisfaction without the delays of courtship. She cites as another cause the commercialization of sex. "To the greedy and artful commercial mind everything can be shaped and compelled into sex patterns. Even laundry soap and shoe polish have their part in the sex dance." [77]

So far five causes have been proposed. Kinsey points to the impact of economic emancipation, the influence of psychoanalysis, and the contact with different sexual codes during the wars. Pearl Buck refers to the habit of swift satisfaction among men and to the commercialization of sex. In addition, in socialist countries the change is usually attributed to a decline of religion.

The impact of the economic emancipation of women seems indeed important. Virginity in women is no longer their chief adornment. Their successes in their professions can also make them attractive. As married women they need no longer tolerate the situation of an unhappy marriage simply because they are economically dependent on their husbands. They can apply for divorce. The influence of psychoanalysis is restricted to the United States where it has had exceptional success. The same holds for commercialization. As for the war experiences stressed by both Kinsey and Pearl Buck, we must note that the most conspicuous changes in sexual morality are changes in the attitudes of present-day youth who did not participate in the world wars. These changes moreover are particularly evident in Sweden, which did not take part in the war. As to the influence of secularization, one should start first by testing its extent. Why is sexual morality so much more rigorous in the Soviet Union than in Poland even though both have been exposed to antireligious propaganda and both have socialist structure? The rigor of the sexual morality in the Soviet Union is expressed in its penal and civil codes. The unwed mother and her child do not have rights equal to those of a legal family, divorce is not easy, abortion is condemned, male homosexuality is punished. Thus neither the social system nor the antireligious attitude on the part of the government can be made responsible for sexual morality. Norway and Sweden which have been reputed to be the first countries in Europe to liberalize sexual morality are not considered especially advanced in secularization.

Thus it is not easy to give an answer to the question, what are the possible causes of the so-called sexual revolution? What is usually called sexual morality constitutes a complicated whole and in order to find a solution to the problem it would be advisable to treat each of its components separately. Special causes are, for example, to be attributed to the indisputable earlier start in sexual life of youngsters of the Euro-American culture. This may be due to the number of stimuli diffused by mass media, which accelerate biological maturity. The attitude toward homosexuals is a different matter. Lack of disapproval of this practice in Japan seems to be the result of overpopulation, which accounts also for the approval of birth control and abortion. A decline in the conviction that sex is sinful could in turn be treated as a symptom of declining religion in countries belonging to Christian traditions.

The last question concerning the so-called sexual revolution is whether it is a revolution of the whole society or whether it affects only a part of it. So far as I know, we do not have at our disposal any comparative empirical research investigating the changes in sexual morality in the middle class and among workers and peasantry. Premarital experiences have always been treated with leniency among Polish peasantry, while adultery is much disapproved. It has been the reverse in the middle class, which was ruthless in condemning the loss of virginity before marriage while admitting clandestine adultery if discreet enough to show respect for public opinion. If one is allowed to guess, I should risk the opinion that the revolution is first of all a middle class revolution.

Let us now review the supposed causes of the increase in juvenile delinquency. We hear and read sometimes about the role of the instability and discord of family life and the growing number of divorces. During a conference on juvenile delinquency held in Washington in 1960, some speakers pointed to the reduction of the family to the nuclear one. A large family, including not only parents but also grandparents and other relatives, was supposed to constitute a "pressure group" which acted as a counterbalance to an excess of leniency on the part of parents. Another factor frequently mentioned was the professional work of women outside the home which did not permit them to give the children the care they needed.

In countries devastated during the war, where the housing problem raised great difficulties, people had to live crowded together in small apartments. In these conditions the home was unattractive and teenagers took refuge in the streets, which did not provide them with the right education.

While some countries were too poor to provide good living conditions, others were rich enough to permit young men to earn substantial sums very early, surpassing the salaries of their parents, which lessened the authority of the latter. This was an explanation which one could hear in Sweden.

In all countries having television there was a general concern over programs which abounded in violence: Westerns and murder stories. Further explanations mentioned the decline of religious faith, the instability of the political situation and the threat of a new war with new means of destruction, the cynicism of rulers who were striving for power, regardless of the morality of means used to achieve this end, and last but not least, the feeling of absolute helplessness noted in surveys of students of different countries.

All these factors may, of course, work simultaneously. As to the question which of them is especially important, we have had more negative than positive answers. We know that the question of whether we have to do with socialism or capitalism is irrelevant,

that the economic status of the delinquent and his social prove-
nance may be varied.[78]

In order to throw light on the problem it will perhaps be
advisable to consult the past. From the *Spectator* we learn that
eighteenth-century England was molested by the so-called Mohocks. Richard Steele characterized them as a

> Nocturnal Fraternity under the title of the Mohocks club, a
> name borrowed it seems from a sort of Cannibals in India who
> subsist by Plundering and Devouring all the Nations about them.
> Agreeable to their name, the avowed Design of their Institution
> is Mischief . . . an outrageous Ambition of doing all possible
> Hurt to their Fellow-Creatures, is the great Cement of their As-
> sembly, and the only Qualification required in the Members.[79]

The Mohocks were accused of attacking all who were so
unfortunate as to walk the streets through which they patrolled.
They committed different acts of brutality: broke windows,
squeezed the noses of people flat to the face, set women upon their
heads, carried a war against all mankind. So far as we can judge
from this report their aggression was not aimed at gain. It was
aggression for the sake of aggression—a trait considered characteristic of contemporary hoodlums in different countries.

CHAPTER III

Theories Concerning Morality
as a Whole

The Origin of Morality

The list of problems concerning moral ideas which I examined in the previous chapter is far from exhausting those which could be included in a sociology of morality. Our cultural heritage has left us a number of general statements concerning morality as a whole. Among the oldest thoughts in this domain are those concerning the origin of morality. We remember that Thrasymachus in Plato's *Republic* contends that morality was invented by the strong, who propagated moral rules for those they governed in order to manipulate them more easily. "Each form of government enacts the laws with a view to its own advantage, a democracy democratic laws, and tyranny autocratic and the others likewise, and by so legislating they proclaim that the just for their subjects is that which is for their—the rulers'—advantage and the man who deviates from this law they chastise as a law breaker and a wrongdoer." [1] This opinion was later upheld by Mandeville, who in *The Fable of the Bees*, attributed the origin of a large part of moral laws to clever politicians, who without them would be unable to control the citizens. An opposing view is represented by Callicles in the dialogue *Gorgias*. He contends that morality was invented by the weak to secure them against the strong. "The weak invented the view that it is something ugly and unjust to strive to possess more than others, and that it is better to be wronged than to wrong." Moral rules were thus intended to disable the strong. This opinion was later on upheld by Nietzsche in his book, *Toward a Genealogy of Morals,* in which he denounced Christian morality as a morality of slaves who defended themselves by its help against their noble masters.

These two hypotheses were usually treated as opposites although each could be adopted for different moral rules. There is no need to ascribe the origin of morality to a single factor. It is probable that the fifth commandment of the Decalogue, "Honor thy father and thy mother, that thy days may be long in the Lord thy God hath given thee," took the point of view of parents addressing their children. Similarly the model of a good child is necessarily obedient. The fact that in England the law against homosexuals, recently repealed, affects only men and does not condemn lesbian behavior, is a proof that it was made by men. When we read a description of a good wife, we usually have no doubt that his description is made by men. In the Human Relations Area Files we find the following description of an ideal wife by the Wolof of Senegambia.

> She should be respectful and obedient to her husband and never quarrel or argue with him. She should keep his secrets, guard his property as her own, and be prepared to give or loan her husband some of her possession . . . when he is in need. She should do many things without being asked, such as washing her husband's clothes, cleaning his house, and being hospitable to his visitors. She should be prepared to do anything she is asked to do, rapidly and well, even if she must do it in the middle of the night. She should be receptive to her husband's sexual advances and, indeed, please him in every way.

If the wife did not conform to this pattern she was expected to be deprived of certain privileges in the afterworld and her children would never be a success.

It is hardly possible to doubt that this ideal was created by men. Its acceptance was very wide since it suited the husband's needs very well and it did not lose its force until the present day.

My last remarks made use of the theory which admits that the origin of moral rules can be attributed to those whose interests they serve. *Is fecit cui prodest* was the old Latin saying adopted in jurisprudence. This theory, as is well known, was revived by Marxists who treated morality as the product of class interests. In his work on three sources and three components of Marxism, Lenin wrote: "People have always been and always will be silly victims of deceit and self-deceit in politics, until they learn to discover under any moral, religious, political, social phrase-mongering, statements and promises, the interests of this or that class." The logical value of this statement depends on the meaning of the ambiguous term "interest." Jeremy Bentham in his *Introduction to the Principles of Morals and Legislation* wrote: "Interest is one of those words which, not having any superior genus, cannot in the ordinary way be defined." To be defined in the ordinary way was, according to Bentham, to be defined by the Aristotelian definition of the *genus proximum* and the *differentia specifica*. Terms which could not be defined this way were called by Bentham incomplete terms, which in order to be defined must be put into a context. Thus Bentham would decline the possibility of defining the word "interest" but would agree in defining a phrase like "X is interested in realizing the state of affairs S." To be interested in something may have a psychological and a nonpsychological interpretation. In the psychological sense, to be interested in something is to desire the same thing. To follow one's interests is in this case to follow one's desires, and to state that in the choice of our ideology we follow our desires amounts to a trivial statement.

The situation is different when the word "interest" is interpreted in a nonpsychological way. We are expected to speak then of the so-called objective interests. In this sense it is in the interest of people to read and write, although the illiterate man may protest against education, and it is in the interests of women to obtain political rights, although they may exhibit no aspirations of this kind. In this sense the opinion that people always follow their interests seems false.

Opinions Concerning the Evolution of Moral Ideas

Next to general statements concerning the origin of morality I will cite descriptions outlining the evolution of morality. The work of Charles Darwin drew attention to this problem. These descriptions were usually not objective. They were based on the assumption that evolution represented a steady progress. Many critical remarks have been made since that time against the point of view they represent. First of all they were reproached for being uni-linear. The development of cultural anthropology has made their position untenable. Nobody today would try to represent the development of morality as a single process in which primitive people are viewed as children and Euro-American moral values are the highest point to be reached.

Another objection pointed to the fact that writers who saw morality as an evolutionary process were confusing facts and postulates. An example is the assertion that there was a transition from heteronomy to autonomy in the development of the individual as well as in the development of mankind. So far as I know nobody tried to verify this theory empirically, while the opinion that very few people reach the stage of autonomy in their personal development seems rather plausible. But if the theorist did not feel any need to verify his contention, this was because it was a postulate rather than a descriptive, empirical judgment.

I have already noted that in descriptions of the evolution of morality writers were rarely aware whether they used the word "moral" in its neutral sense, opposed to "non-moral," or whether in the sense opposed to "immoral." In the first case, the development of morality would constitute the development of norms and evaluations of a given kind, while in the second case it would involve the development of conduct deserving approval. Most writers had the second use in mind. When they inquired about the sources of morality, citing examples of mutual aid or sacrifice observed among animals (Kropotkin) or when they attributed morality to the fact that we cannot satisfy our needs without the help of others (Feuerbach), they referred to factors which could explain why people show a tendency to overcome their egoism. They regarded egoism itself as understandable without comment.

While it is impossible to outline the evolution of morality in contemporary complex societies without taking into account all the factors which contribute to its differentiation, one can watch, either directly or through historical documents, some definite changes taking place. The England which we know from Samuel

Pepys' diary and even into the eighteenth-century exhibits some moral traits quite different from those which we find in Victorian England. A researcher who wishes to study a definite change finds his task is much easier when there is only one center propagating moral patterns, as is the case in contemporary socialist countries.

A Polish sociologist compared the content of a very popular Polish weekly paper addressed to women in the years 1950–1951 with that in 1956–1957.[2] In 1950–1951 the heroines of short stories published in this paper were mostly of peasant or worker origin. They were usually depicted in their professional work, which was decisive for their position in the family and for their sexual attractiveness. Their emotional life was scarcely taken into account. Procreation was an important task in the family and the professional life of the mother was not supposed to conflict with the task of rearing numerous children. The education of the children and the handing down of tradition had to be done outside the family in governmental institutions such as nurseries or Montessori schools.

By 1956–1957 the ideal picture of the family had undergone considerable change. The heroines of short stories now belonged to the intelligentsia. The professional life of women was treated as much less important. Women were shown first of all as wives and mothers, the focus of the emotional life of their families.

In this kind of research we cannot tell anything about the moral convictions and ideal patterns of the readers. We can only learn something about the change in the patterns propagated, not whether they are adopted and integrated by the readers.

There are theorists who contend that while social changes within a society can provoke the development of new ideals of personality, these new ideals can also come from without and be diffused by imitation. To this opinion one used to reply that modes of conduct coming from without would never be assimilated unless they corresponded to vital needs already in existence. This opinion, although convincing, does not explain certain phenomena. Since the time of the Revolution France had a very influential middle class, while Poland did not. Yet the fierce attack of French writers like Maupassant on middle class morality found a ready response in Poland. Romanticism with its revival of chivalric ideals and its opposition to philistinism overran many European countries in spite of their different social backgrounds.

Functionalism Applied to Moral Norms

In his explanation of moral rules, Montesquieu, who may be said to have been the first sociologist of morality, tacitly implied a certain thesis that has been supported by his successors right up to the present day. Formulated roughly, his thesis was that every moral rule or social custom serves a need. For example, Montesquieu attributed the polygyny found in certain societies to the fact that these societies had a surplus of women. In such societies polygyny was able to satisfy the sexual needs of a larger number of women than monogamy could have done. In other cases, according to Montesquieu, polygyny was connected with the rapid aging of women in a hot climate. Here polygyny was to the advantage of the men, who felt the need to replace their old wives with younger women. Later authors explained polygyny by referring to economic needs and showed that in some kinds of economies it was advantageous to have many wives. In still other societies, where the chief had the privilege of being able to keep more than one wife, this form of polygyny gave him recognition and prestige. While the theory of interests was concerned with the origin of moral rules, the theory of needs was concerned with their function.

Similar explanations may constantly be found in modern authors. Durkheim, in his paper on the definition of moral fact ("Détermination du fait moral" included in Durkheim's *Sociologie et Philosophie*, Paris 1951, p. 81) contended that every society has on the whole the morality which corresponds to its needs.[3] It has often been said that Puritan morality suited the needs of small business men, but no longer suits the needs of white collar workers, who have had to adopt other personality patterns. There are anthropologists who point out the usefulness of different superstitions and declare that these superstitions could not have survived unless they had satisfied some need of the groups which held them. Clyde Kluckhohn, for example, in his book on witchcraft among the Navajo Indians, tries to show that their practice of magic reduces their anxieties and at the same time canalizes their tendencies toward aggression. "Any cultural practice," he says in another place, "must be functional, or it will disappear before long." [4] Here, "to be functional" means to be "eufunctional" as opposed to "dysfunctional," and the satisfying of needs means the satisfying of rational, accepted needs.

The same opinion was expressed by Bronislaw Malinowski, who sometimes gave it the form of an empirical thesis which said that every moral rule, or more broadly, every custom, always serves some need. On another occasion he formulated this opinion in a methodological postulate and enjoined research workers to look for this need by observing how a rule functions in a given society.

I am not interested here in the methodological postulate but in the empirical thesis. Its logical value depends entirely on the concept of "need." If the word "need" is taken in a wide sense, this thesis cannot be falsified and is thus theoretically sterile; if "need" is understood in a definite narrow sense, the thesis in a general form is false.

In the first and wider sense, need, like interest, is a psychological concept. In this sense everyone who desires something has a need. When the word is given this meaning we can see, if we try, a need behind every custom, and behind every rule which recommends the observance of this custom. Some authors have rightly pointed out that when a particular society forbids premarital sexual relations, this ban serves the need for healthy temperance among the members of that society. In a different society which approves of premarital sexual relations, this tolerance allows people to make a sensible choice of marriage partner and lessens the risk of choosing on the basis of temporary physical passion.

Thus when need is understood in the psychological sense, the view that every custom corresponds to some need cannot be disproved. Therefore theoreticians frequently understand the concept of need in a definite, non-psychological sense, and assume, for example, that man's needs (conscious or not) are the fulfillment of conditions necessary for his survival. Individual survival is biological survival; but when we speak of the survival of a group the matter is not so simple, for it is obvious that this may mean biological survival, or survival as a cultural entity, or survival as a separate and independent political entity.

Let us consider the biological survival of the group. If the functionalist theory were true, rules of conduct particularly important for the survival of the group ought to be emphasized. We can, however, observe that there are societies in which practices detrimental to the group are not disapproved, and that some societies attribute great importance to rules prohibiting conduct comparatively innocuous or adopt rules disastrous for their very existence.

Ward Hunt Goodenough in his book *Cooperation in Change* informs us that the women of Yap in the Pacific Ocean continue practices that have contributed to the progressive depopulation of their island. Abortions in order to avoid early motherhood constitute a common practice and this leads to infertility.[5] From other authors we learn about societies where lack of maternal care does not encounter disapproval. One remembers the Greek practice of exposing infants, or the treatment of children working in factories as described in *Das Kapital*.

Everyone is familiar with the view that family unity is absolutely indispensable for the health of society and that societies where family bonds have become slackened lose their power of resistance and sooner or later succumb to invasion and annihilation. In the light of this view it is surely strange that in many societies such a social institution as primogeniture has survived for centuries without moral opposition. The inheritance of the father's entire fortune by the eldest son certainly did not encourage family unity, but the need for family unity has had to give way to the father's need to pass on the results of his life's work to his successor. If the fatal effect of some customs were to arouse the opposition of society, alcoholism would be denounced with particular severity, whereas in actual fact the public usually looks on the drunken man with a tolerant smile. The ban on incest is stressed on a particularly wide scale and with a force that is out of all proportion to its effect on the survival of an individual or of the group, at least in those cases where the concept of kinship is extended to include more distant relatives or people whom we would not consider kin in the accepted sense.

In all the 250 societies widely dispersed on the globe from which George Peter Murdock gathered his information, the incest taboo applied universally to all persons within the nuclear family.[6] Sexual intercourse was nowhere permissible between mother and son, father and daughter, brother and sister. The author agrees with modern geneticists in contesting the supposed biological harm of close inbreeding as the explanation of this taboo. Inbreeding may be harmful, but it may also be positively advantageous. Besides, why would this taboo be adopted by a tribe ignorant of the fact of physical paternity?

Murdock's opinion is tenable insofar as he tries to explain the strength of the taboo and the horror at the idea of its transgression by the disruptive force of sexual competition within the nuclear family,[7] but why should the taboo be extended beyond the immediate family or even beyond any biological kinship? Murdock invokes the help of psychoanalysis, of sociology, cultural anthropology, and behaviorist psychology in order to respond to this question. But I am not interested here in the question of how this taboo originated but in whether the emphasis on moral rules is proportional to their importance for the survival of the society. In many cases of incest taboo the endeavors to find a rationale in the strength of the prohibitions fail, while elements of pure convention are conspicuous. Hamlet considers the marriage of his mother with his uncle to be incestuous, while in other cultures marriage to one's widowed sister-in-law constitutes an obligation.

These examples show that customs are not always dependent on whether they encourage survival. This independence comes out still more clearly when we consider the chivalry ethos of the Middle Ages, which for several centuries kept up rules and customs which were absolutely fatal for the biological survival of individuals or groups.

Let us begin with the code for knightly combat. It is sometimes said that this code consisted of rules which were in fact never followed in practice. This is not true. Undoubtedly the code applied only to combat between knights who were equal in rank, but it was a code which really was observed. Its effects were disastrous because it sacrificed elementary strategy for honor. In 1213 a battle took place at Muret between Simon de Montfort, leader of the Crusade against the Albigenses, and Peter II, King of Aragon. Simon de Montfort had much smaller forces and he saw that it would be impossible for him to defeat the enemy, who were in tents behind fortifications. He was therefore anxious to lure them into the open fields. Peter II himself came to his aid for, not wanting to be thought a coward, he scorned the chance to fight from a privileged position. He therefore ordered his men to leave their entrenchments. But this was not all. Simon de Montfort also planned to kill the king himself. The latter again facilitated his plan. Having exchanged arms with another knight, he was fighting in the thick of the battle. The knights belonging to Simon de Montfort at once threw themselves on the knight bearing the king's arms. At this, Peter sprang to the aid of the knight who was under attack, shouting "I am the king!" When he was killed the knights surrounding him let themselves be massacred rather than retreat and abandon his body. Simon de Montfort, who was hated by the people, won a complete victory.[8] The code of chivalry to which Peter II subscribed remained in force for several centuries longer. Even at the battle of Fontenoy in 1745 the French allowed themselves to be beaten by the English through sheer gallantry.

Not only rules of combat, but a system of values as well, which was nurtured by certain strata upholding the traditions of chivalry, showed surprising longevity despite the fact that their influence led very largely to disaster. Right up to the last war, the Polish gentry[9] stubbornly despised not only trade but also farming for profit. Just before the war, a landowner who had an estate on the outskirts of a large town decided to concentrate on growing vegetables which would find a ready market in the town. His neighbors thereupon referred to him contemptuously as a trades-man and spoke of him almost as if he had betrayed his class. This attitude to the land greatly reduced its productivity. The landown-ers were continually short of cash and their properties became more and more neglected. Considering the fact that Poland was an agricultural country and that a large proportion of the land belonged to the gentry, their contempt for thinking in terms of profit was necessarily fatal not only for them but for the whole country as well. Yet this attitude was hard to kill and it was only finally removed by postwar social changes. Thus the functionalists' thesis, that moral rules or social customs serve the survival of the individual or the group, must be restricted in its application. And if the thesis ceases to be general, the sociologist begins to be faced with the necessity of demonstrating each time that it may be applied in a particular case.

It has already been observed that the functional theory, which treats norms as serving the needs of a given community and more especially its need for survival, forced itself upon cultural anthropologists who studied primitive cultures where the question of survival was particularly important and where the comparatively simple structure of the society permitted them to speak about needs which were common to all its members. But what Robert King Merton called the postulate of functional unity of society does not work in more complicated social structures. In turn, the tendency to explain in a rational way the existence of each norm, in his opinion, constituted an exaggerated reaction against the theory of cultural lag.[10]

I do not wish to enter here into details concerning functionalism in general. All Merton's critical remarks are relevant in the case of functionalism applied to moral norms. Thus we often have to do here with a confusion of purpose and function, the confusion of intended and unintended effects of a norm, and with the tendency to see things as black or white. The old creed of the Stoics that good can beget only good and evil can only result from evil was a conviction which satisfied moral needs.

Cultural Relativism in Morality

The ethnocentric orientation of authors who, in outlining the evolution of morality, were convinced that their hierarchy of values was the best, provoked an opposition known as cultural relativism. From the standpoint of cultural relativism it is not possible to criticize values adopted in a given culture from one's own point of view, because that point of view is also culture-bound, culture-determined. As Redfield puts it, "cultural relativism means that the values expressed in any culture are to be both understood and themselves valued only according to the way the people who carry that culture see things." [11] Melville J. Herskovits, the chief partisan of cultural relativism, affirms that we cannot evaluate cultural values comparatively, since any attempt at comparative evaluation presupposes an ethnocentric perspective.[12] The need for absolute values is also culture-bound. It is impossible to argue reasonably that monogamy is better than polygamy.

Bronisław Malinowski, in his lectures at the London School of Economics in 1934–1935, repeated the argument of a Trobriander who learned from him that a great war was going on in Europe and that in a single battle near Verdun the number of men killed was so great that it would be possible to cover with their corpses the atoll where the Trobriander lived. He looked at Malinowski incredulous and doubted this information, saying that it was quite impossible to eat so much flesh. When Malinowski explained that there are no cannibals in Europe, the Trobriander burst into indignation. "Is it not a shame to kill so many people for no use!" Malinowski quoted this story in order to show that even from an ethnocentric point of view, it was not always clear whose moral opinions represented the higher level.

Cultural relativism has been treated not only as a reaction against ethnocentrism but also as a consequence of functionalism. As functionalists considered all customs as serving some reasonable need (we remember Durkheim's opinion that "chaque société a la morale qu'il lui faut"), a *laissez faire* attitude seemed to them advisable. This attitude, however, had to be confined within limits. So long as cultural anthropologists had to do with small cultural units which did not represent any danger to anybody, they could advocate tolerance. But should they adopt the same attitude in the case of Hitler's crematoria? [13] This well-known argument was not easy to refute.

The same Herskovits who professed a radical cultural relativism and denied the existence of supracultural values required a respect for the dignity inherent in every body of custom, the right of men to live in terms of their own traditions. This right was obviously treated as a supracultural value and the respect recommended was a supracultural duty.

The Problem of Universal Moral Standards

THE TOPICALITY OF THE PROBLEM

The question whether there are any universally accepted moral standards is of long standing. It recurs throughout the ages, becoming now and then a subject of more or less animated discussion. Twice in modern times we have witnessed an intensification of interest in this problem. Both eighteenth century and modern scholars seem to consider it to be a matter of topical interest, although in each epoch they do so for reasons of their own. In his *Essay on the Human Understanding* John Locke denies the existence of commonly accepted "practical" rules. He refuses to admit their innate origin, believing the human brain to be a *tabula rasa* at birth. The universality of practical rules being a necessary condition of their innateness, he who denies the existence of the former must simultaneously deny the existence of the latter. The question of the universality of moral standards reappears in Locke's writings once again, but this time he reaches another conclusion. The very existence of universal moral standards serves him this time as an argument in favor of the assertion that morality is prior to Christianity and the Revelation. The acceptance of certain religious dogmas is neither indispensable nor sufficient to allow people to profess and practice certain moral laws. To prove this assertion it is enough to cite the instance of the high morality of the Chinese people who know these truths and put them into practice even though they are not Christians. Universality, therefore, refuted at one time as a condition of innateness, is accepted at another time by Locke and used by him to prove that, in spite of differences in religious faith, there are moral feelings common to all people. The latter view is expressed in his *Reasonableness of Christianity*. Christ is presented here as a great reformer and systematist of laws held in common by all people long before his time. Each of these contradictory opinions was directed against traditional religious views: one refuted the belief in a divine spark with which every human soul was said to have been inspired, while the other claimed that morality was not unique to Christianity since the highest and most perfect standards of morality are also found among non-Christians.

In our own times the question of universally accepted moral standards arises occasionally. The problem had lost much of its importance for ethnocentrically minded scholars who cared little for universality because they believed that eventually their own scale of values would be absorbed by all societies. The belief of these scholars that only their own moral opinions were true was shaken by thinkers who rejected the assumption that moral norms and value judgments could be true or false. That denial of their logical value caused people to return to the idea of universality, seeing in it support for their own convictions. That point will be discussed in a later part of this study. Various other theoretical and practical causes have enhanced the topicality of the problem.

In an epoch that is characterized by a violent breach of fundamental moral rules, people seek eagerly for evidence to prove that their moral laws have evolved from some universally and deeply felt needs of all men. Bertrand Russell wrote that the cruelties perpetrated by Nazism made it impossible to assume the attitude of *de gustibus non est disputandum*.[14]

This resorting to universally accepted moral standards was also bound up with definite tasks, such as those which were set forth by the Nuremberg trial. The conception of the law of nature was revived at this trial: it was admitted that there were moral convictions shared by all people. This was necessary in order to sit in judgment over war criminals whose crimes had not been foreseen by makers of international law.

Finally, the universal character of moral norms and value judgments has sometimes been stressed by those who protest the claim that they have been formulated solely to serve the interests of the ruling classes. In every such case discussions on universal moral standards have been mixed with strong emotions. The frequently recurring question, what is the sense of human life, must usually be interpreted as a question of whether good will triumph in our world. That question in turn implies that judgments concerning good and evil are common to all.

It is quite evident that an answer to the question of whether there are some universally acknowledged moral standards and values can only be found empirically by recurrence to facts. Comparative studies have already been undertaken to seek that answer. Yet the difficulties that the specialist must face are considerable and it will take time before any satisfactory results of this research are produced. If one wants to find an answer—he must make clear to himself precisely what meaning he assigns to the term "universal," as well as to the term "accepted."[15] The word "universal" must have time and space limits for it is impossible to deal with the opinions of all the people who have ever lived on earth. Quite naturally, therefore, we shall not attempt to recreate a fully detailed picture of the past, especially since only a minute part of our heritage has been recorded in writing.

Consequently we must concentrate on modern times. Should we impose on our epoch restrictive limits of space? Let us assume that we have done so and have decided to examine only our own society. We may ask then whether universality should require absolute unanimity or should it merely stand for the consent of the majority. Locke excluded children and idiots. Those entitled to voice their opinions on the subject were those who could comprehend norms and values.

Now a few words about the term "accepted." Long ago Locke knew that it is one thing to accept the statement that the earth moves around the sun and quite another to accept practical principles. In order to show that there are no generally accepted practical rules Locke insisted that the word "accepted" should mean not only the conviction that a given rule was right but also that it was followed in practice. In view of this demand he easily convinced the reader that universally accepted standards do not exist. In our considerations we may provisionally assume that only the man who condemns cases of violations of norms accepts those norms.

ATTEMPTS AT AN A PRIORI SOLUTION

Those interested in the question have paid little attention so far to these preliminary points of primary importance in reaching an empirical solution. They could disregard them as they discussed the problem in a purely abstract way. One of their a priori suggestions asserted that the obviousness of certain norms and values is clear to everybody. Another argued that moral norms are shared by all because they satisfy basic needs which are common to all people. Let us examine these two propositions.

1. When we state the obviousness of some norms and values, their obviousness may have a dual nature.

    a. It may be due to lack of precision in the wording of the

statement. In this case it can be nothing else but pseudo-obvious-ness.

   b. It may denote genuine obviousness that has nothing to do with the moral character of the statement.[16]

   (Ad a) Let us consider pseudo-obviousness first. A well-known slogan says that every man should be given the conditions in which he can develop all his capabilities. The general acceptance of this truth will stop when we ask whether we really do mean *all* capabilities. Should we promote the development of an ability to exploit or to humiliate? It appears now that we tacitly assumed, "all his good capabilities." But this restriction would require general consent as to which capabilities are good ones.

   "We must try to achieve the happiness of all," is another highly convincing slogan of wide popular appeal. Dupréel has pointed out that the word "happiness" is frequently supplemented in people's minds by the word "true." [17] And when speaking about true happiness every man implies his own vision of happiness and his personal pattern of excellence. Let us recall here the acrobatics found in John Stuart Mill's *Utilitarianism* when he tries to prove that virtue is "part" of happiness. Similarly, every attempt to fill out the idea of happiness with some substantial context will tend to annihilate obviousness and at the same time the general acceptance of this general tenet.

   "*Neminem laedere*" appears in many textbooks on ethics. Yet what do we mean by *laedere*? Locke advocated mildness in educating the children of the privileged classes, for whom above all his work *Some Thoughts Concerning Education* was destined. At the same time he proposed that the children of poor parents be kept together in a shelter where they were to work, and be fed on bread and water, with a little gruel heated on the stove that was to warm the room during the winter. In Locke's opinion this treatment was not at all harmful; on the contrary, he maintained that it was beneficial for the children. This example is given here because the law that forbids treating helpless children badly is frequently cited as one of the obvious and generally accepted rules.

   (Ad b) Now I should like to point out two varieties of genuine obviousness. One is implied by the tautological character of the statement. The other, although not tautological, is also an obviousness of nonmoral character.

The element of tautology has always been considerable in ethics and although stressed by many authors it still deserves some additional remarks.

In his *Principia Ethica*, G. E. Moore considered all sentences with the predicate "good" as self-evident, though synthetic. Yet if we look more closely into the definitions that appear in ethical studies, we can easily notice an abundance of value judgments which ought to be considered analytic. How, for instance, do we proceed when we construct a definition of egoism? Usually we reject the assumption that he who seeks his own good is an egoist, as there is nothing wrong with a man going to a concert or hurrying to the dentist to get his aching tooth anaesthetized, although in both cases he is seeking his own good. We call a man an egoist who seeks his own interests against the interests of others. Thus we restrict the denotation of the word "egoism" so narrowly that it falls in with the opinion that egoism is bad. When we have done so, what is our condemnation of egoism if it is not a tautology? Likewise, when defining veracity we determine the range of its denotation until it embraces positive values only. Not every statement, even when it conforms to reality, is a manifestation of veracity, but only that one which conforms to reality and costs us something. Thus to say that veracity is good is nothing else but the mere wording of the emotional content of the word.

Some scholars propose as an undoubtedly universal and commonly accepted standard the one which bids solidarity with one's own group. That standard seems to imply two possible meanings: either it is self-evident and therefore tautological, or it is not self-evident and thus loses its convincing force. What in fact can "my group" or "one's own group" really mean? If "my group" is one I have joined of my own free will, then I have felt solidarity with its opinions or activities. In this case the solidarity principle is tautological. If, on the other hand, "my group" means, for instance, "the group in which I was born," like the caste of a Hindu determined at birth, then our principle is no longer tautological but, for a European, at least, neither is it binding.

Out of numerous tautological norms and value judgments that have already been cited as self-evident by various authors, it is worth mentioning here one more statement which has been quoted as a supposed synthetic and yet self-evident value judgment. The example is to be found in an article by Paul Weiss called "The Universal Ethical Standard." It reads, "It is absolutely and always wrong to kill a friend deliberately and wantonly." The author adds that this statement plays in ethics the same role as the following assertion in ontology: "It is absurd that some day in some place I shall meet myself coming toward me." [18]

Disregarding the fact that one can hardly imagine an action undertaken "thoughtlessly and for no cause whatever," it seems to me that we cannot possibly deny the tautological character of the quoted sentence. "What sort of friend is that whom one kills deliberately and wantonly?" any unbiased reader will ask, feeling the presence of some inner contradiction in this statement. A friend is a person whom by definition we must wish well.

There has already been mentioned another kind of self-evidence which like the self-evidence of tautology is not of a moral kind. It springs from other sources. Let us suppose that in a certain kindergarten a game is played with the children. During the game the youngest among them up to the age of four are to receive extra toys. The daughter of the teacher is an older child, having already passed the age limit and for this reason she cannot have an extra toy. Yet because of her mother's position she is treated as an exception. This illustrates a violation of the principle which says that if a variable has a determined range it must always assume the same value. Each "x" and only "x" receives a toy. The "x" denotes a child up to four years of age. The teacher's daughter is outside this specific limit and therefore should not be given a toy.

In his study of justice, Charles Perelman gives to the principle of justice the form of a syllogism of the type "Barbara." [19] That syllogism reads: All A's should be B's. M is an A. M should be B. The evidence of this principle is analogous to that of the *dictum de omni et nullo* and is not evidence of a moral sort.

A similar principle of consistency is meant by the well-known principle about "clean hands." It rules over the very procedure of evaluation and forbids the pot calling the kettle black. What has been tacitly admitted here? It is that like actions should get like blame. Again, if we think this rule self-evident, this evidence does not seem moral.

ATTEMPTS AT AN EMPIRICAL SOLUTION OF THE PROBLEM

We have already examined the attempt to give a positive answer to the question, whether there exist universal moral standards, by referring to the assumption that moral norms together with other social norms serve to satisfy at least the basic needs, the needs common of all people. This opinion is professed by cultural anthropologists who have an instrumental conception of culture.

According to the interpretation of the word "need," as I tried to show above (p. 104), this statement may be either a sterile truism which cannot be falsified or a false statement.

Alfred Louis Kroeber, in his article, "The Morals of Uncivilized People," stresses similarities considering that "the moral element is basically instinctive. . . . Being an inherent element of the human mind, it is psychologically unexplainable." The author treats as instinctive the repugnance toward murder, appropriation of the possessions of others, treachery, want of hospitality, and incest, the last abhorred equally by philosophers and the crudest savages.[20]

In the study entitled "The Common Denominator of Cultures," G. P. Murdock discusses cultural differences and similarities.[21] According to him, the first have received more attention, perhaps because they are more immediately obvious. But cross-cultural similarities are farreaching, although they consist not of details but of categories. "What cultures are found to have in common is a uniform system of classification, not a fund of identical elements." Thus, all cultures have cleanliness training, division of labor, food taboos, greetings, a way of mourning, and so on. All people seem essentially alike in their basic psychological equipment. But to ascribe human conduct to basic drives is to oversimplify complex social phenomena. Derived, acquired drives are of great importance. Education, for example, is not supported by a primary drive. We have to look into the principles of learning for an interpretation of the universal culture pattern and take into account the existence of common stimuli, stimuli like night and day, darkness, rain, sneezing, breathing, childbirth, sickness, and death. In any learning situation the number of possible responses is limited. The nuclear family is always an economic unit charged with child-rearing, socialization, and early education. The common denominator of cultures is to be sought in the factors governing the acquisition of all habitual behavior and among these the most important is reward.

Kroeber's remarks are not persuasive. I leave aside the use of the concept of instinct, criticized so convincingly by L. L. Bernard,[22] since it can be replaced by another, less controversial concept. What is more important is the fact that neither the repugnance to appropriation of the possessions of others nor the repugnance to killing seems universal. As to Murdock's theory, the fact of the existence of common categories due to common psychological equipment and to common stimuli is indisputable, but it is not this kind of similarity which ethical writers and cultural anthropologists are looking for.

In his study called *Objectivity of Norms*, cited above, Arne Naess enumerates factors which work for an overestimation of similarities and those which work for their underestimation. Supplementing some of his suggestions with my own, I should like to count among the factors working for overestimation: 1) the tautological character of norms and their vague and general formulation; 2) the egocentric and ethnocentric attitude of the researchers, who impute to others their own reactions and adjust concepts to their own conceptual repertory; 3) the tendency of the persons interviewed to answer questions so as to please the researcher. As factors contributing to the underestimation of similarities I wish to point out: 1) a tendency to see a difference of moral opinions in the difference of customs, although different customs may well be connected with an identity of moral attitudes. Thus different habits of mourning are associated with a common belief that one ought to show grief after the death of one's relatives. 2) An insufficient taking into account that the differences may lie in the strategy for reaching certain goals, rather than in the goals themselves; 3) an insufficient taking into account of the possibility that the difference may be due to different beliefs, while looking for universally accepted moral values we look for differences, in spite of a common factual basis.

In conclusion I must cite Naess' reasonable advice to avoid generalities, as the likelihood of coming across generally accepted moral norms is much greater for definite commands or prohibitions than for vague and general ones. Agreement can probably be reached when the command "Do not kill your father" is concerned. The probability is lessened when the general prohibition "Do not kill" is tested in different cultures.

UNIVERSALITY OF MORAL STANDARDS AS COMPARED
WITH UNIVERSALITY OF OTHER STANDARDS AND
OF DESCRIPTIONS

An emotional approach to the problem of the universality of some moral standards is, as we know, more striking than it is to the question of universal aesthetic norms. Many people assert that the former are universal, while the latter are of great variety. Let us consider what factors bear upon the difference in these attitudes.

The fact that there are no universal tastes even within one social group seems to be obvious. Paul switches off the radio whenever classical music is on the air. On hearing his neighbor's radio broadcasting his favorite melody, John switches his radio on, greatly displeased with himself for having failed to catch the first bars of the tune. Your furniture may become the object of vigorous disapproval freely expressed by your friends, although you know them to belong to the same social group as yourself. A wide range of colors is a striking feature in women's dresses and every woman thinks she is right in her choice.

The lack of unanimity of opinion in matters of beauty is caused not only by obvious divergence of taste, but also by the fact that we are not especially interested in having aesthetic norms and values commonly shared by everyone. On the contrary, people endowed with a keen sense of beauty fear the boredom which might be caused by the spread of European culture, facilitated by modern means of transportation. Travelling might lose much of its attraction were we to find in every country the same motifs in art or music. Still, a tourist who goes on a journey in order to find new and unexpected stimuli in the world of colors and tones, prefers to find in the exotic lands where he travels the principle "thou shalt not kill" fully respected, especially in its version, "thou shalt not kill tourists."

Within the same culture variety of tastes has often been used to show one's own superiority. In class societies this difference has been employed to guard members of one class against the transgression of social barriers. As everybody knows, the lower classes imitate the fashions of the upper classes, who in turn guard their privileged position by means of new fashion.

Variety of taste is usefully employed in trade. Europeans made good use of it during the colonial period in bartering cheap notions for ivory. Even today various sorts of shoddy goods or those out of fashion are sold in the colonies.

Several other examples can be given to prove that a variety of tastes can further many practical ends. It would be much more difficult to find similar instances in the sphere of morality. We seem far more interested in having moral opinions shared by all people. One can hardly imagine any instance of peaceful cooperation among groups or within one group if even one member does not accept the obligations which the others share.

To a certain extent, some kind of universality is a necessary condition of the binding force of ethical standards. Hobbes was aware of this fact when he added to the laws determining a peaceful cooperation of citizens the restriction that they are binding only if others obey them too. The rule "thou shalt not kill" loses its obligatory force when we are assaulted by someone who wishes to strangle us.

It has already been mentioned that our search for universality of ethical standards used to be bound up with the necessity for finding some support, since the logical validity of the principles could not be relied on. Here too we see the great differences between beauty and moral good. The sphere of beauty is largely the domain of art. In art there are specialists who can act in doubtful cases. No plebiscite is needed here. Specialists pass judgment on a monument and may decide whether it should be erected in their town and where. We can acquire certain historical knowledge and skills which make us better judges of art and better able to compare aesthetic values. A judgment expressed by an art or music specialist carries more validity than the opinion of a layman. In moral matters this is hardly possible. Conscience is attributed to all men. Pointing to a philosopher as a specialist in moral matters arouses doubt as to who is the greater authority in such matters: a man of blameless conduct who has never bothered to reflect on the subject, or a man who acts as a signpost, although he does not practice what he preaches. In moral matters the very choice of the judge is a case of moral decision, while the choice of an authority in the field of art is not a matter of aesthetics.

Now let us examine our final point, namely the question, why the problem of universality is non-existent in descriptions, in the same form as we find it in the sphere of moral standards.

Although we may endeavor to treat as invariant the observations that lie at the basis of experimental sciences while the person of the observer is changed, yet nobody cares to assess the logical value of empirical statements by falling upon their universality nor resorting to a plebiscite. When we say, "Notre Dame in Paris has two towers," we assume that this observation must be accepted by everybody who understands the words used and who has seen the cathedral. The statement, "Notre Dame is the most beautiful church in France," is another matter. In *The Fable of the Bees* Bernard de Mandeville maintained that nothing would prove better the incorrectness of his opinions than their acceptance by the majority of men. This opinion was repeated after him by Voltaire. It expresses the belief that the universality of one's own views does not confirm them. Who would like to prove that the earth moves around the sun by circulating a questionnaire?

A theoretician frequently takes universality as evidence that values are objective in the sense that they are a quality of the valued object. If each man judges an action in the same manner, no matter what his tradition and upbringing, it is because good and evil is in that action and is not a mere projection of capricious emotions. Alf Ross has shown that thus conceived objectivity, as applied to judgments of perceptions at least, must not necessarily go with universality. Two kinds of wine may objectively differ from each other, although this difference may not be universally stated since it can be discovered only by winetasters, that is, by exceptional men. Their opinion is confirmed by the fact that the chemical components in one kind of wine differ from those found in the other. In such a case we follow their judgment against the opinion of the majority of people. Even if there were large numbers of color-blind people, we should support an objective conditioning of the qualitative difference in the perception of red and green colors by the difference in the length of the waves serving as their stimuli.[23] There leads only one way from universality to objectivity, namely, when we identify one with the other, taking subjective values as the expression of personal whims.

Against those who seem to invalidate the standing of values by showing that there are fewer universal opinions in the sphere of evaluation than perception, C. I. Lewis in defense of value judgments maintains that this difference is only apparent and due to the fact that differences in perception usually come to light only by accident, as for instance, when we learn by accident that our friend is color-blind. Besides, the differences in evaluation are, in his opinion, more striking because they are in a greater degree reflected in action.[24]

Neither of these observations seems to be correct. We have frequently to do with divergences in perceptions, and they need not be illustrated with such examples as the above case of color-blind people. One man may see a twin star in the sky where another man will see only one. One man feels cold on entering a room, while another will say it is quite warm. On entering a house, one man, again, will alarm everybody by saying that a gas pipe is leaking; another visitor will smell no gas at all. It is not in the number of divergent opinions that we see the difference between perceptions and evaluations. The number—let me state that in passing—can hardly be an object of comparison. As far as perceptions are concerned we have at our disposal a variety of methods by which we can obtain a unanimity of opinions. No such methods are applicable to values. If we see a twin star, we can convince our opponent who sees only one by letting him scan the skies through a telescope or binoculars. Divergent opinions as to the warmth or coldness of a room can be checked by examining a thermometer. The only remaining point of controversy will then be the question of whether one likes to live in a cool or a warm house. These two attitudes can be expressed in two introspective sentences, which cannot be contradictory because each is speaking about something else.

In the sphere of evaluation, as we know, when the difference of opinions concerning facts is removed, the only means of bringing our opponent to an agreement is by his emotional reeducation. While there is no reason why we should doubt a potential universality of perceptions, notwithstanding every possible distinction in cultural background, universality of evaluations seems closely bound with their levelling. Against Lewis' comment that a difference of evaluations is a more striking one because it is revealed through action, I must point out that differences in perception are no less influential upon our activities than are differences in our valuations.

When comparing moral valuations with descriptions—as regards their universality, I have tried to show that the latter would be neither a characteristic of the truth of our valuations nor of the objectivity of value as a quality proper to the things. Nevertheless, there is no doubt that an empirically proved universality might have great emotional significance. It might strengthen our conviction that moral values express, indeed, men's most essential needs and that all mankind can reach understanding without losing specific features of particular cultures. Thus comparative studies to this effect are worthwhile and should be continued. But researchers must be encouraged to move faster, since modern methods of transportation and communication may establish universalization through uniform standards of education. This situation would make it impossible for us to resolve our problem of universality which was to be a universality in spite of cultural differences.

Cultural anthropology, as the mirthless joke of some specialists goes, is gradually acquiring distinct features of entropology, because nowadays the principle of entropy finds its application more and more in the sphere of culture.[25]

General sociological problems concerning moral rules are, of course, not exhausted by discussing their origin or their function. It would be interesting to watch how norms are enforced in a given society, what it means to accept a norm and to internalize it, what sanctions are prevalent in a given group in the case of transgression, and how some transgression can be institutionalized, constituting what was called countermores by Lasswell and Kaplan.[26]

CHAPTER IV

The Nobility Ethos and the Bourgeois Ethos

The Homeric Warrior

In the second part of my considerations I gave a very rough account of factors which influence morality. In the final part of this book I should like to dwell a little longer on the ethos of the nobility and the ethos of the middle class, two different value orientations attributed to different class positions.

In order to draw a picture of the nobility ethos we must begin with ancient Greece. Numerous are the sources from which it would be possible to reconstruct this particular way of life, but I shall confine myself to Homer and to Aristotle's description of the magnanimous man.

Homer's heroes are first of all distinguished by their noble lineage. Most of them have gods as ancestors. Birth, wealth, and power decide the position of a man in the social hierarchy. A high rank is necessary to be *agathos*. The approval associated with this word can even be bestowed on people whose conduct is disapproved, as in the case of Agamemnon when he deprived Achilles of the slave girl.[1]

Homer's heroes are strong and beautiful. I stress this last point because men representing an ideal of personality in the middle class ethos will not be required to be beautiful. They will only have to look *respectable*, while beauty will be an attribute of

women. Paris' conduct in his fight with Menelaus would be evaluated differently if his beauty were not so disarming.

Homer's warriors are marked by their refined language which
shows them immediately to be among the *agathoi*. The king of the
Phaeacians knew at once by Odysseus' speech that he had to do
with a distinguished guest. Language since that time has always
constituted a class criterion.

Homer's world is a world of plenty. Nobody is preoccupied
with economic troubles. War is the chief way of acquiring wealth.
Menelaus supervises a large estate, but his wealth has been
brought in by ships. When Odysseus, after his return to Ithaca,
finds his chests emptied by Penelope's suitors, he decides to fill
them again with booty obtained from a new war expedition. The
fact that Penelope's suitors could live at the expense of Odysseus
for twenty years in an atmosphere of perpetual feasting is proof
that the wealth accumulated in these chests was substantial. Trade
is despised by Homer's nobility as a mean occupation.

Thorstein Veblen, in his description of the leisure class, cites
four occupations which do not degrade a man: government, warfare, religious ceremonies, and sports. Homer's heroes confirm this
observation. They reign, fight, honor the gods with sacrifices, and
are champions in games. To handle disci or bows skillfully is a
mark of class superiority, as leisure is needed to acquire these
techniques. When Odysseus, still unidentified, watches the games
at the court of the Phaeacians, the king's son, intending to probe
the social status of his father's guest, challenges him to compete.
When Odysseus answers that, searching in vain to return to his
home, he is too sick at heart to think of games, one of the
competitors goes so far as to insult him, saying that he is probably
nothing but a sailor belonging to a merchant ship. Then Odysseus
picks up the largest discus of all and without difficulty overshoots
the marks of all the other throws. His social position is established
by this achievement.

Homer's warriors are constantly preoccupied with distinguishing themselves. Each book of the *Iliad* constitutes a story of deeds
proving someone's excellence (*aristeia*) which must be duly appreciated by others. The warriors are fascinated by what F. Znaniecki

called "reflected ego," that is, the opinion (*timē*) they enjoy among their equals. Achilles chooses a short but glorious life. Hector expects to gain fame from his son. When deceived by Athena and certain of his doom he decides that he will not die ingloriously but will perform some deed that will ring through the ages.[2] These are values which Adkins called competitive values, as opposed to cooperative values which are required of women. Any evidence that one is being evaluated below one's merits constitutes an offence and leads to revenge. Nothing is more degrading than to be ridiculed. Ajax, blinded by a fit of anger, loses his honor by attacking a flock of sheep, taking it for a detachment of Atrides, and has to commit suicide. The French historian Hippolite Taine, an admirer of aristocracy, wrote: "In the middle and lower classes the chief motive of conduct is self-interest. With an aristocracy the mainspring is pride. Now, among the profound sentiments of man there is none more apt to be transformed into probity, patriotism and conscience, for a proud man feels the need of self-respect, and to obtain it, he is led to deserve it."[3] The pride of Homer's heroes, however, could not exceed certain limits because it could hurt the pride of the gods, who were no less vulnerable in this respect than men.

Of reasons leading to war, two were most important: for revenge, and to obtain booty and slaves. Victors killed all the men from the opposite camp, while slavery was the lot of the women and children. O. R. Sandstrom finds in Homer the following rules governing the conduct of war: spare the suppliant, respect the herald, honor the truce, allow the burial of the dead and refrain from boasting over the slain. These rules were probably due to mutual utility and in part to pity. "Spare the suppliant" could also be attributed to a prospect of gain: it was more profitable to obtain a ransom than to kill.

It was indeed a lasting custom to decide battles by a duel since as late as 1938 Japan was told to propose to China the solution of their conflict by a single fight. Opponents in the *Iliad* sometimes begin by glorifying each other, each extolling the other's noble lineage and manifesting mutual respect. This is so in the case of Diomedes against Glaukos or Hector against Ajax. The glorification of the foe may express the solidarity binding among equals, in spite of the conflict, but it may also exhibit a desire to enhance one's own glory as future victor.[4] Sometimes the opponents start by insulting and depreciating each other.

The warrior could make his situation more dangerous in order to demonstrate hs valor. Thus Diomedes leaves his chariot to fight on foot. Hitting one's adversary from behind was quite admissible and thus only wounds acquired on the front of the body were honorable. Stripping off the armor of one's vanquished adversary was considered justifiable. Respect for the aged, however, restrains Achilles from doing it when Andromacha's father is concerned. Archers were not held in esteem. This was perhaps due to the fact that the bow was the weapon of people of a lower status, a weapon which could be used from a safe distance and which could injure only a warrior without armor. Poisonous arrows were strongly prohibited. In sport one could not compete with a person whose capacities were unequal to one's own, especially with a host to whom one owed gratitude for hospitality as did Odysseus in the court of the Phaeacians.

The qualities expected from Homer's heroes were primarily qualities of a good, that is, successful warrior. Courage, strength, and skill were required not only in wars for booty or for revenge but also for fights settling minor differences. It was observed long ago that the word *nomos* is not used either in the *Iliad* or in the *Odyssey*. In a quarrel there was no appeal to justice. Might was right in Homer's world and the punishment of crimes was a private affair. Adkins is of the opinion that Homeric valuation is made in terms of success and failure. Mistake is not distinguished from moral error, intentions are not important.

In time of peace Homer's ruling class enjoyed leisure. The king of the Phaeacians describes to Odysseus the way of life in his court in the following words: the things in which we take delight are the lyre, the dance, clean linen, a hot bath and our bed. Work was done by crowds of servants whose number enhanced the prestige of their master. Penelope, we remember, was attended by fifty maidservants. A number of parasites was also included in the court.

The attitude of Homer's heroes to the lower classes is very interesting. As has already been observed, people of mean birth are presented in two main roles. When portrayed sympathetically, they usually belong to the category of faithful servants. The old nurse of Odysseus, who first recognizes him after his return to Ithaca, may serve as an example. She comes from a noble but poor family, which confirms the fact that merit and noble birth are closely associated with each other. Thersites, the man of humble origin who urges the soldiers besieging Troy to give up fighting and return home instead of shedding blood for private quarrels, is described as a hateful creature. He squints, he is lame, almost bald, and hunchbacked. Ugliness and wickedness will for centuries to come be ascribed to people of low rank, with the exception of faithful servants. In the French *fabliaux* of the Middle Ages the descriptions of villains follow Homer's description of Thersites almost word for word.

The Homeric warrior must be hospitable and generous. Achilles reproaches Agamemnon for keeping the largest part of the booty for himself. The hero must be unobtrusive in his hospitality and must respect the privacy of his guests. Odysseus' incognito is respected at the court of the Phaeacians. No one presses him to reveal his name. A knowledge of the world derived from numerous travels and adventures is duly appreciated. Both men and women show their feelings in an exaggerated way. Men shed copious tears. Achilles indulges in his famous burst of anger. I stress this point because we will see a change in this respect in the models of the nobility later on.

So far we have been concerned only with the male ideals of Homer's aristocracy. It is time to add a few words about women. Homer's nobility live under one roof in great families of a patrilineal structure. The father of a woman is her master until her marriage; her husband assumes this role after marriage. In their absence the eldest son decides her lot, as Telemachus decides Penelope's fate. Still, the position of women is not as bad as it will be with the growing influence of the East. The advice of Arete, the wife of the Phaeacian king, is much appreciated by her husband. Nausicaa is known not only for her beauty but also for her wisdom. Of course, chastity before marriage and fidelity to her husband constitute a woman's chief virtues. It must be noted that women of high birth did not spend their time in leisure. Arete is always busy with her household. Her daughter helps her servants in washing clothes. I stress this point because a wife functioning as mere decoration will be a requisite, not of the nobility, but rather of the European upper middle class of the nineteenth century. I make this remark because Veblen's book does not sufficiently take into account female ideals and their transformations.

The attitude of men toward women is not without gallantry. When Nausicaa's father scolds her for not accompanying the stranger on his way to the court, Odysseus immediately assumes the blame, although Nausicaa had been concerned for her reputation.

The way of life praised by the Homeric warrior differs greatly from that recommended by Hesiod in his *Works and Days*. Hesiod was not particularly interested in questions of birth. He did not think of distinguishing himself, but was absorbed in securing for himself a decent living by honest toil. He did not expect anything valuable from war and praised the peaceful life. When wronged, the Homeric warrior relied upon himself for compensation. Hesiod, who complained that his brother took more than his share of the property left by his father, expected justice from Zeus. In his opinion, virtue was not acquired by birth but by hard work. In his relations with his neighbors he was not guided by magnanimity but by the principle *"do ut des."* Help your neighbor in his need because some day you may be in need yourself. In his choice of a wife he was not sensitive to beauty. He appreciated a woman's virtues as a diligent and frugal housekeeper.

Werner Jaeger in *Paideia* affirms that it was only the nobility who created ideals of personality, difused in the course of time among the lower classes, and that the Greek nobility was the first to make a conscious effort to mold the life of the society. Both these statements are doubtful. Every society brings up children according to a picture of what a man should be, and in complex societies these pictures are different. Jaeger's opinion is suggested by an ethnocentric attitude. The word "culture" is used in the singular, as there is only one culture which deserves this laudatory name—his own.

"Homeric values . . . suit Homeric society, inasmuch as they command those qualities which most evidently secure its existence." [5] This is the opinion of A. W. H. Adkins whom we have already quoted several times. This functionalist statement suggests some reservations. Homeric society was not monolithic and while one can contend that the glorified values supported the nobility, they did not serve the interests of those who, like Thersites, did not wish to shed blood for private quarrels. "The type of man most needed was most admired," we read in the same author. Most needed by whom? Were people like Hesiod interested in wars for revenge or prestige?

Homer's poems have been so frequently discussed that it is not easy to make a new contribution to the subject. But I could not refrain from starting with these remarks in order to show the similarities which contributed to the formation of a picture of the nobility ethos as a typological unit.

Before leaving Greece I must recall the description of the magnanimous man given by Aristotle in the *Nichomachean Ethics*. The *megalopsūchos* is concerned with honor. He claims much and deserves much, having good ground for his pride. Greatness of soul is related to great objects. He who possesses it will not engage in many undertakings, but only in those that are important and distinguished. Thus he is always willing to face danger, but only in a great cause. He likes to confer benefits, but is ashamed to receive them because to do so is a mark of inferiority. He is not prone to admiration, as nothing is great to him. He likes to own beautiful and useless things, rather than things which are useful, because the former show his independence more. The vulgar man, Aristotle contended, is not motivated by a sense of honor and avoids evil from fear of punishment, not because of its baseness.

The picture of the magnanimous man impressed many generations of people who could afford this lofty attitude. As we see, it was an ideal of personality for peacetime and its war-addicted admirers had to supplement it by a greater emphasis on prowess. M. Greaves, in her book *The Blazon of Honour*, follows the description of the Aristotelian *megalopsūchos* through centuries of English literature and shows its influence on the concept of gentleman. "In the pagan world, the man who founded his pride on his own worth was following the highest that he could attain." [6] "Aristotle's values are almost exactly the reverse of middle class

Puritan values," observes C. B. Watson, having in mind the *megalopsūchos*.[7]

The Nobility in the Middle Ages

Although some historians have cast doubt on the similarities between the ethos of Homer's warriors and the medieval knights, we are entitled to expect analogies because in both cases we are dealing with the way of life of a privileged class whose main activity is fighting.

Analogies due to a similar class position and to a similar occupation have also been observed between Germanic tribes as described by Tacitus in his *Germania* and the medieval knight. Although Tacitus was idealizing his picture in order to give his readers *exempla recti*, his work is nevertheless a valuable source of information.

Joined in the service of a chief, the Germans were bound to defend him, to risk their lives in his defense, and even to ascribe to him their own heroic deeds. It was regarded as shameful to give up one's shield, and the warrior who did not fight with enough courage was in such disrepute that he was forced to commit suicide. These people considered war as the only occupation worthy of man. They despised merchants. To cultivate land and wait patiently for the harvest was not, according to them, an occupation which would allow people to be magnificent. On the other hand, they liked to bestow gifts, neither counting what they gave nor feeling obliged by what they received.

Battles between Franks and Arabs persuaded Charles Martel that infantry cannot stand against cavalry. According to R. L. Kilgour, he decided to enable his men to buy horses and coats of mail and in order to do so he confiscated church lands and gave them to his followers. This was the beginning of the feudal system. In order to belong to this privileged group of warriors a man had to be strong, able to carry the weight of the armor, expert in horsemanship, and skilled in the use of weapons, especially the lance and the sword.[8]

So far as I know, historians are in agreement as to the fact that the formulation of a moral code by medieval knights was rather late and was connected with the growing importance of the middle class, which constituted a threat to the privileged. This code was expected to justify their privileged position and to form a barrier not easily crossed by newcomers. When successful in crossing this barrier, the newcomers were quick to stress the role of the code and of an elaborate etiquette.

Here is the picture of an ideal knight as outlined by E. Deschamps, a prolific author of ballads, born in 1346:

> You who would win the order of knighthood must lead a new life; devoutly you must watch in prayer, flee from sin, pride and baseness; you must defend the Church, and succor the widow and the orphan; you must be bold and guard the people; loyal and valiant taking nothing from others: thus should a knight conduct himself.
>
> He should have a humble heart, should always strive to follow deeds of chivalry; loyal in war he should be a great traveler, should attend tournaments and joust for his fair lady; he must strive always for honor, so that he may not be touched by blame nor be accused of cowardice; and among all men he should deem himself the least: thus should the knight conduct himself.
>
> He should love his rightful lord and above all guard his domain; he should have generosity and be an honest judge; he should seek the company of valiant knights, in order to hear and learn from all their words, and to understand the prowess of the brave, that he himself may perform mighty deeds, as formerly did king Alexander: thus should a knight conduct himself.[9]

This is a code formulated in the fourteenth century. It is possible to extract principles of knightly behavior from earlier sources—from legends circulating in different versions and related not only in courts but at places where pilgrims used to stop and rest. Referring to these legends I will review the main traits required of a medieval knight.

In principle the knight had to be of noble birth. We know that this condition was not always fulfilled. A man could acquire nobility by warlike skill and by purchase, but medieval society was strongly hierarchical, even among the knights themselves. In the legends lower classes were treated as non-existent. In descriptions of battles no mention was ever made about the way ordinary soldiers were fighting. Only the fights between nobles were taken into account.[10] If the villeins played any role, like the guardian of wild bulls near the magic fountain in Chrétien de Troyes' *Yvain ou le Chevalier au Lion,* they were described like Thersites in the *Iliad.* Low origin was associated with ugliness and meanness of character.

The strength of the medieval warrior can best be illustrated by the fight of Beowulf, a Scandinavian hero, with the monster Grendel. Grendel was constantly threatening the Danes. It crept from its cavern in the night and killed the king's favorite followers. Beowulf, hearing about the plight of the population, arrived from a distance to offer his services. In order to make his task more difficult and his merit greater, he fought barehanded with the terrible monster. After killing it he did not keep the treasures guarded by the beast, but gave them all to the king as a true knight ought to do.[11]

A knight was expected to test his valor constantly by glorious deeds. When Yvain marries the wife of the knight whom he has killed, his friend Gauvain urges him to leave his lady in order to seek opportunities for new battles. "Think first of all about your renown" ("Songez d'abord à votre renommée"). It is indeed the first thing the knight is concerned with. Roland will not blow his horn and ask for help when he realizes his hopeless situation, because he is afraid of being thought a coward. He sacrifices his men, and his best friend, Oliver, to his pride. The language of the Knight makes use of a term equivalent to the Greek *ubris,* namely, *desmesure.* Like Homer's heroes the knight is absorbed by his "reflected ego," by what people think of him. "There is no use to behave well, if one does not wish to make it known"—this is the opinion of the knight Yvain.[12] All medieval legends demonstrate this insatiable pride.

The knight must be conscious of the fact that he belongs to an elite. He is bound to solidarity with its members, even when they happen to be his adversaries. During a battle between the Franks and the Saracens, Ogier le Danois is challenged to a duel with a noble knight representing the foe. When Ogier is caught in a treacherous way by the Saracens, his noble adversary, disapproving of treachery and feeling solidarity with his opponent, gives himself up to the Franks in exchange for Ogier. After the conquest of a castle the common people were killed, while noble prisoners were often treated like honored guests. In one medieval legend, a soldier boasted that he had succeeded in killing a noble enemy. His superior ordered him to be hanged for his impudence.[13]

The fraternity of arms, which I have tried to illustrate, did not prevent the nobles from carrying out the duty of revenge for any real or imaginary offense. Battles described in medieval legends usually originated from vindictiveness. While family bonds in the nuclear family were rather loose—the knight absent in search of adventures, the sons from the age of seven brought up at courts—the whole kin took offense when one of its members was not duly respected. On the other side of the coin, when Roland's stepfather, Ganelon, was proved by ordeal to be a traitor, all his relatives were hanged with him.

Needless to say, a knight had to be brave, magnificent, and hospitable. The wandering troubadours of the legends were interested in praising magnificence because they were supported by gifts. Largesse has for centuries been considered evidence of noble birth.[14] We remember that Achilles reproached Agamemnon because he took much for himself and distributed little.

The knight had to keep his oath despite any adversity. Huizinga relates that King John the Good, after the escape of his son who was serving as a hostage in England, went to England himself, leaving his country to the perils of another regency. It was a common practice to make strange vows which had to be fulfilled at any cost. A group of warriors made a vow never to fly from a battlefield at a distance greater than fifty acres. Ninety knights were killed because of this oath.[15] But the obligation of keeping promises was binding only between equals.

Last but not least, the knight had to be loyal to his lord, had to defend him, if necessary at the cost of his own life, had to protect widows and orphans, and be true in love to his fair lady. Lancelot was extremely reluctant to fight with his lord, King Arthur. Yvain freed three hundred virgins who had been kept prisoner and terribly exploited. He also defended a virgin who had been deprived of her inheritance by her evil sister. True love was appreciated in men as well as in women. Lancelot was praised for being the truest of lovers, and Queen Guinevere, wife of King Arthur, "because of her unfaltering love for Sir Lancelot was to end her days honorably and with sweetness," [16] in spite of the fact that their love was adulterous.

Chivalry was at first a military class within a society divided into those who fight, those who pray, and those who work. When we speak of chivalry today we usually mean a complex attitude toward an enemy, toward the weak in general, and toward women in particular. These were the essentials in the chivalric legacy of the Middle Ages. I will dwell a little longer on these two points.

The code of fair play which was binding in a fight between two nobles originated in pride, respect for the adversary due to class solidarity, and an attitude of play. Self-respect and the need for gamesmanship did not permit the killing of an unarmed enemy. Lancelot deplored the fact that he had killed two unarmed knights in the thick of battle. He expected to repent it until his death and offered as atonement to make a pilgrimage on foot, wearing only a shirt.[17] It was shameful to kill an enemy overthrown from his horse. "I will never strike a knight who has fallen," exclaims Lancelot. "God defend me from such dishonor!" [18] Victory under these conditions was too easy to enhance one's glory. In addition, a spirit of play motivated the knight, when he wanted to have an equal partner. Not only was it not meritorious to win a fight with an unequal adversary; there was no fun in fighting under such conditions. This is why it happened so often in legends that the knight who overthrew his adversary dismounted and continued fighting on foot.[19] Similarly, an experienced tennis player finds no pleasure in playing with a beginner. The practice of making chances equal before starting a battle is well known to cultural anthropologists. Sumner and Keller cite instances of primitive Australian tribes who provide their enemies with weapons in order to make chances equal.[20] In the feuds between Pisa and Florence, when one town had its fleet destroyed by a storm, the other was supposed to wait for its reconstruction before declaring war.

Not to be suspected of cowardice was the knight's first concern, more important than questions of strategy. A knight wearing his coat of mail could not retreat. For this reason, says Huizinga, a knight riding in reconnaissance could not wear his armor.[21] To risk one's army and its victory for personal reasons has sometimes

been called individualism. Thus Achilles was called an individual-
ist when, motivated by anger against Agamemnon, he risked the
destiny of the army besieging Troy for personal reasons. The word
"individualism" will change its meaning when it is attributed to
men of the Renaissance who aimed at a full expansion of their
personality.

I will pass now to the attitude of the knight toward women.
This attitude was one of gallantry and adoration. The fair lady was
usually a married woman and this is why some authors contend
that "gallantry was nothing more or less than conventional adultery and socialized bigamy." [22] Love was treated as a factor enno-
bling a man and working for his excellence.

> "S'élever doit par sa Dame
> celui qui l'a pour maîtresse ou femme,
> sinon il est juste qu'elle ne l'aime plus
> privé de valeur et de gloire." [23]

The victor as such proved to be more excellent than the vanquished
and it is therefore no wonder that the wife of a knight killed by
Yvain was easily persuaded by her maid to marry the murderer.
When two knights measure their strength in a single combat,
argued the maid, whom would you appreciate more: the victor or
the defeated? For my part I prefer the first. The lady thought this
argument convincing and the marriage was celebrated immediately after the funeral.

I will return to the question of gallantry when I discuss its
relation to the teachings of the Church. For the present I shall
review different hypotheses which attempt to explain this cult of
women of high rank as expressed in the legends.

Chivalric love is not a cause but a symptom of the new
position of women in society, says the well-known art historian, A.
Hauser.[24] Some people, however, deny the rise of the prestige of
women in the Middle Ages. All this gallantry and adulation was,
according to them, a game in which women were really "kicked
upstairs." In fact, the dominion of women in love was connected
with their complete dependence on their husbands in every other
respect. The husband was expected to be a servant in love, but he
was the lord in marriage.[25] A wife, when her adultery was proved,

was burned at the stake. It is true that at the last moment a lover might arrive to prove her innocence successfully, but in principle she had to be punished, while the knight could safely indulge in illegal liaisons.

Other historians of the Middle Ages, treating this cult seriously, are of the opinion that it was an extension of the idea of service. Whoever served the lord assumed a similar attitude toward his lady. Still others say that the cult was invented and fostered by women themselves. The obstinate faithfulness required from men served the interests of the ladies who, taking advantage of the frequent absences of their husbands, usurped the reverence and loyalty due to them for themselves. Another, still more skeptical explanation attributes the idea of this cult to minstrels who wandered from castle to castle and, finding the lords usually absent, flattered the ladies on whom they depended for hospitality and for gifts given on leaving. In their ballads they extolled magnificence in the hope of a return.

Not all explanations of the phenomenon which interests us are so matter of fact. The fictions in which adulation of women abounded could be half-conscious, constituting a game which satisfied the yearning for an ideal far from being realized. It is possible also that the refinement of courtly love was intended to distinguish the nobility from the vulgar and to oppose the Church with its tendency to degrade love experiences.[26]

All these factors could work, of course, simultaneously. Their list was sometimes completed by historians, who pointed out the possible influence of Arabian poetry or of Ovid's *Ars amandi*, and the influence of monasteries in which monks and nuns exchanged letters full of exaltation, characteristic of love at a distance, consumed in imagination.[27]

One does not have to wait for the development of the middle class to find severe criticism of the discrepancy between the chivalric code and everyday practice. Knights were criticized by churchmen, by minstrels, by the bourgeois, and by some knights themselves. They were criticized for their cupidity, for stealing cattle, sheep, and oxen, robbing churches and travelers. They were accused of empty vows and vain challenges, of debauchery, wifebeating, dueling without respecting the rules of fair play. Hostages were not respected, ransoms which ruined the prisoner were required, tournaments were treated, not as a noble game, but as an occasion to take from the vanquished his horse, his armor, and his weapons.[28] If we encounter in Malory the sending of a woman to the enemy camp as ambassador, it was probably because male ambassadors were not trustworthy enough. One of the authors of ballads deplored the fact that knights were ashamed to be learned. The education of a knight was certainly not extensive. A boy was sent to court when he reached the age of seven.[29] He had to get some skill in the use of weapons, in fencing, riding, hunting, playing chess. But knights often did not know how to read and had to send for a clerk in order to learn the contents of a written message. Malory's King Arthur had to ask for such clerical help.[30]

Although the Church tried to make the knight subservient to its aims, the moral code of the knight was in disagreement with the teachings of the Church. Pride was extolled instead of humility, vengeance was urged for every real or imaginary insult. There was no respect for human life. "A life of murder and debauchery," writes Kilgour, "could be expiated in a monastery, or if this entailed too much discomfort, the knight's body might be wrapped in a monk's habit after death." [31] The superficiality of Christianity in the knight's convictions and conduct and the constant clash of two different moral orientations can constantly be seen in the legends. In principle, adulterous love was condemned, but in practice all sympathies were on the side of the lovers. God obviously shared this attitude since judicial duels ended, as a rule, in a complete victory for sin, a victory obtained by fraud. The cases of Iseult and of Queen Guinevere can serve as examples. Iseult was called to certify in an ordeal that she was not guilty of adultery and had to prove it by lifting and keeping in her hands a blazing iron bar. By the help of an oath, verablly adequate but in fact false, she stood the test and lifted the bar, showing her hands intact. In spite of his adulterous love for Guinevere, Lancelot was seen by the archbishop in a dream borne by angels through the open gates of heaven, and from Lancelot's body after his death rose a sweet aroma. Knowledge of their adultery could not prevent either King Arthur or King Mark from loving the sinners.

For Kilgour the waning of chivalry begins with the late

thirteenth century. The last tournament in England took place during the coronation of Queen Elizabeth I, but this was simply a game in which knights of bourgeois origin fought in armor richer than a noble knight could have afforded. The decline of chivalry was accompanied by a very elaborate etiquette,[32] a practice typical of a declining class who, by observing complicated rituals, tries to keep a rising lower class at a distance. This passionate regard for formalities was also certainly an expression of an aesthetic and a ludic attitude. "The whole chivalric culture of the last centuries of the Middle Ages," writes Huizinga, "is marked by an unstable equilibrium between sentimentality and mockery." [33]

Many factors contributed to the decline of chivalry. In 1313 gunpowder was invented, changing the role of the knight who was used to fighting the enemy in hand to hand combat. The efficiency of fighting no longer depended on skill in handling weapons. Everybody could be taught to manipulate a gun. Another invention made the coat of mail not so safe as it had been before: it could now be pierced with a bullet. Besides, the coat of mail was not practical. It was extremely heavy and hampered the knights in their movements. A knight who fell could not rise again without help. There were also important economic reasons which contributed to the lowering of the knight's position. A devaluation of money ruined the barons. The king looked for support from the bourgeois in his struggle against the knights for power. He reserved for himself the right to make knights, while the privilege of the nobles to wear certain rare furs, silk, or other ornaments was more and more bestowed on the middle class.[34]

The efficiency of knights as warriors was dubious in comparison with the growing importance of the infantry. France was defeated in several battles with England because the union of the infantry and cavalry proved very successful in the English army. Instead of appreciating the help of the infantry the French treated it with contempt. At the battle of Agincourt in 1415 the French cavalry "refused the service of 6000 archers sent by the city of Paris, saying 'Quel besoin avons nous de ces boutiquiers?' " [35] In an earlier battle in 1302 the knights dismissed the infantry out of jealousy because it proved too successful. As Kilgour shows, Froissart, the well-known chronicler of the time, delighted in ridiculing the French burghers and peasants whenever they tried to take part in war.

In spite of the fact that the chivalric ideal was far from being realized, it had a great importance for posterity. It influenced international law, contributed to the formation of the ideal of a gentleman, was revived in the Romantic period, and did not cease until the present day to be an ideal of fair fighting. In his book *Human Society in Ethics and Politics*, Bertrand Russel writes:

> Although its manifestations were often absurd and sometimes tragic, belief in the importance of personal honour had important merits, and its decay is far from being an unmixed gain. It involved courage and truthfulness, unwillingness to betray a trust and chivalry towards those who were weak without being social inferiors. . . . When the conception of honour is freed from aristocratic insolence and from proneness to violence, something remains which helps to preserve personal integrity and to promote mutual trust in social relations. I should not wish this legacy of the age of chivalry to be wholly lost to the world.[36]

The Courtier

Contemporary historians are, so far as I know, unanimous in denying that there is a gap between the Middle Ages and the Renaissance. Most of them consider that Burckhardt overestimated the change, when in fact there was a continuous development and many traits thought peculiar to the Renaissance were already present in the Middle Ages. According to Huizinga, "the thirst for honor and glory proper to the men of the Renaissance is essentially the same as the chivalrous ambition of earlier times, and of French origin. Only it has shaken off the feudal form and assumed an antique garb." [37]

When speaking of the decline of chivalry I stressed the growing importance of the court and the lessening role of the knights as warriors. This change contributed to the transformation of the former warrior into a courtier. I will begin with the picture of the ideal *cortegiano* as presented by Castiglione. His book appeared in Italy in 1528 and was translated into English in 1561. Its numerous successive editions constitute a proof of its popularity.

Castiglione expects his courtier to be of noble birth. Noble birth is advisable because it gives a better start. A noble is by birth endowed with attributes which must be earned with difficulty by somebody who is not noble. This is why one can require from a noble more than from a vulgar person. The courtier must be handsome, not too tall, and full of grace. The only profession suitable for him is to bear arms. He must be successful in different games which need training and dexterity. He must pretend to do everything with nonchalance, without any visible effort, as if everything were easy for him. People will say as they watch him, What could he achieve, if he gave himself the trouble! His speech cannot be vulgar. Castiglione requires a much more extensive knowledge from his courtier than a knight was expected to possess. He must know the languages of antiquity, have a general orientation in the humanities, and be endowed with a refined aesthetic taste. He must be acquainted with music, but he must never perform in this field or in any other as if it were his profession. Whether he plays an instrument or dances he must behave like an amateur. In playing games he must know not only how to win but also how to lose.

The reputation of the courtier is to be his main concern. He is expected to know how to make himself duly appreciated. It was advisable for him not to cheapen himself by appearing in society too often. Whenever a courtier must take part in a social gathering where he is not known, he must manage to make his renown known ahead of time to those he expects to meet. He must be modest in behavior and dress in a way suitable to his rank. His task in company is to please everyone and to make the occasion go smoothly. This topic is treated at length in the *Cortegiano*. It is obvious that participation in court functions constituted the chief occupation of a courtier.

The list of virtues required of a man of the Renaissance was taken from Cicero and combined with the virtues of the Aristotelian *megalopsūchos* which exercised a great influence at that time. Thus prudence or wisdom, justice, fortitude, and temperance, recommended by Cicero, were supplemented by magnanimity or greatness of soul, liberality, magnificence, modesty, courtesy, honesty, and integrity. This ideal was purely secular. Like the portrait by Aristotle, it was an ideal of a proud, independent man whose modesty had nothing to do with humility.[38]

Moral worth was still connected with social status. It was shown in the ambiguity of the word "noble," which meant noble birth as well as moral worth. This monopoly of the privileged was to last for centuries. As late as 1891, Thomas Hardy, in attributing a noble character to his heroine of *Tess of the d'Ubervilles*, could not refrain from representing her as a descendant of a gentle though impoverished family.

From the Italian *cortegiano* we pass to the French ideal of the man of civility (*l'honnête homme*), represented in the seventeenth century by Chevalier de Méré (1610–1685), who left us a written code of what he considered true civility.[39] He was a man of noble birth, conversant with the best Parisian society, an habitué of the court, which he admired and thought the most splendid in the world.

While other courts abound in men absorbed in their professions, in the French court, "there were always idle men, without any profession, but not deprived of merit, who thought only of having a good time and of being duly appreciated by others. . . . They were usually people of a delicate spirit and a tender heart, people proud and courteous, bold and modest, neither mean nor ambitious, not eager to govern. . . . Their only aim was to bring joy all around and their principal care was to deserve esteem and to be loved." [40]

In order to be a man of civility one must be wellborn and have an excellent education together with a knowledge of life, an intuitive understanding of other minds, and a refined taste. The company of women is sought in order to polish and make graceful one's manners. Even virtue must be shown in appropriate measure. Chevalier de Méré does not like severe and intransigent virtues. The virtue which he praises must be amiable and soft. Even honorable people who obstinately stick to their principles are often ridiculed. Moralizing is not advisable: it has the flavor of hypocrisy.

Virtues are to be praised only so far as they contribute to our happiness. Temperance preserves our health, courage is needed in order to defend people who have been wronged, and justice assures peace. Virtues cannot be easy to acquire as only what is difficult is meritorious. *L'honnête homme* must strive for glory but without demanding attention from others.

Chevalier de Méré has not much to say about family life. He is rather against marriage. He feels unity with his class throughout the world and considers *l'esprit bourgeois* provincial and narrow.

The ideal of the courtier was the object of criticism in the same century in which it was delineated. In Shakespeare's play *As You Like It*, the conduct of a courtier is characterized as follows: "I have trod a measure, I have flattered a lady; I have been politick with my friend, smooth with mine enemy; I have undone three tailors; I have had four quarrels and like to have fought one."

In the eighteenth century the word "courtier" has in most cases a pejorative taint. In the *Spirit of the Laws* by Montesquieu we find the following picture of a courtier:

> Let us recollect the conversations and sentiments of people of all countries, in respect to the worthless character of courtiers; and we shall find that these are not airy speculations, but things confirmed by a sad and melancholy experience.
>
> Ambition with idleness, and baseness with pride, a desire to obtain riches without labour, and an aversion to truth, flattery, treason, perfidy, violation of engagements, contempt of civil duties, fear of the prince's virtue, hope for his weakness, but above all, a perpetual ridicule cast upon virtue, are, I think, the characteristics by which most courtiers in all ages and countries have been constantly distinguished." [41]

In spite of this pitiless criticism it is still possible to find instances where the word "courtier" was used in the eighteenth century without any pejorative taint. Such is the case in the letters of Lord Chesterfield to his son, to whom he was giving advice in preparation for his admission into the court. His son was expected to excel in everything he undertook, to be motivated by a "noble thirst of glory." "Content yourself in mediocrity in nothing," repeated his father. While the *cortegiano* was taught to ride horses and to manipulate a lance with dexterity—remnants of the chivalric tradition—Chesterfield does not even mention fencing. He requires only dancing, necessary to develop grace, which is indispensable to please in court. [42] "If you do not please the court you are sent to, you will be of little use to the Court you are sent from.

. . . Please the eyes and the ears, they will introduce you to the heart; and nine times in ten, the heart governs the understanding." "A look, a gesture, an attitude, a tone of voice, all bear their parts in the great work of pleasing." [43] "The Graces, the Graces! Remember the Graces!" [44] While excelling in everything his son was reminded to be never considered as "the literati by profession," as it was not the right way to shine and to rise in the world.

Although both de Méré and Chesterfield stress the art of pleasing, their aims are different. De Méré wanted to please in order to bring joy all around; Chesterfield wanted to please in order to rule. This is why he recommended reserve and self-control in his letters. While Homer's heroes expressed their emotions in an exaggerated way, while medieval knights shed torrents of tears on every occasion and fainted whenever it was the easiest solution to a difficult problem, Chesterfield's courtier was always composed and self-possessed. *Qui nescit dissimulare, nescit regnare* was the motto for a man who must manipulate people, for a man who had renounced government by the sword and who preferred to rule by dextrous diplomacy.

While de Méré characterized his *honnête homme* by idleness, Chesterfield prepared his son to be active as a member of Parliament or as an ambassador to a foreign country. Diplomacy was a suitable occupation for a man of high birth. It was not salaried and thus could be undertaken by aristocrats, whose dignity would not allow them to be recompensed for their services and whose wealth enabled them to pay their own way. Traces of aristocratic traditions can be seen in diplomatic protocol up to the present day. I have in mind hunting parties organized by diplomats who no longer own great estates abounding in game.

That the aristocracy was born to rule was taken for granted by Chesterfield. In his letters he warned his son to avoid any activity not suitable to his rank. He was forbidden to laugh because laughing is vulgar; he was forbidden to hurry because only tradesmen hurry. Chesterfield advised his son to associate with ladies in order to become polished, but otherwise his attitude toward women was rather cynical. Chesterfield did not expect much from family. As to religion, he considered it to be a "collateral security" to virtue, while his religious convictions amounted to a vague belief in a Supreme Being. He regarded an appearance of being religious as indispensable to success in society.

The nobility ethos in eighteenth century England was also described by Lord Shaftesbury. Here again it is of value to distinguish oneself by excellence and to have the kind of virtue which can be acquired only through good breeding and a prolonged education. "It is undeniable . . . that the perfection of grace and comeliness in action and behavior can be framed only among people of liberal education." [45] Shaftesbury calls the ideal of personality *virtuoso*, a name which stresses the role of taste in the achievement of excellence. "It is not merely what we call principle but a taste which governs men." [46] According to him, even conscience will make but a slight figure where taste is amiss. The *virtuoso* is a man of the elite who plays the role of a connoisseur in the consumption of goods. He need not think about securing his existence. He may devote himself to the art of living in a refined way. The notion of duty does not play an important role in Shaftesbury's moral system. Virtue is spontaneous and taste makes law.

Compared to the French ideal of a man of civility, the English noble had a higher sense of responsibility for the life of his country. Shaftesbury would not have praised an idle life spent in good society and concerned primarily with making oneself lovable. He attributed great importance to what he called a sense of partnership with human kind. If he himself did not join more effectively in the social and political activity of his country, this was partly due to poor health which kept him out of town.

Lord Shaftesbury had a very critical attitude toward chivalry. Everything which characterized the Middle Ages was considered "gothic" or barbarous by eighteenth century England. Shaftesbury wondered how people of that time could enjoy tales about monsters killed by brave knights and how women could assume the role of judges in brutal fights. Chesterfield did not approve of Homer's heroes. In his opinion, Achilles was "both a brute and a scoundrel." [47] He did not hesitate to expose his troops to defeat because of a private quarrel and killed people basely, all this knowing that he would be perfectly safe without any armor except a horseshoe fixed to his heel.

There is no need, I think, to multiply examples of nobility ideals of personality in order to persuade the reader that they exhibit throughout the ages striking similarities. These similarities suggest the possibility of discerning a type of morality, a particular ethos, which will stand in relief when compared later on with middle class ideals. Let us refer once more to Montesquieu in order to characterize briefly this typological unit.

According to Montesquieu, the existence of nobility is closely connected with monarchy. "No monarch, no nobility—no nobility, no monarch." [48] In a monarchy honor "sets all the parts of the body politic in motion." [49] Honor supplies the place of virtue:

> The virtues we are here taught, are less what we owe to others, than what we owe to ourselves; they are not so much what assimilates us to, as what distinguishes us from our fellow citizens.
>   Here the actions of men are not judged as good, but as shining; not as just but as great; not as reasonable but as extraordinary. . . . With regard to morals, I have observed that the education of monarchies ought to admit a certain frankness and open carriage. Truth therefore in conversation is a necessary point. But is it for the sake of truth? by no means: truth is requisite only because a person habituated to veracity, has an air of boldness and freedom. . . .
>   . . . The education of monarchies requires a certain politeness of behavior. Men born for society are born to please one another.
>   But politeness rises from a desire of distinguishing ourselves. It is pride that renders us polite. [50]

A few decades earlier Bernard Mandeville wrote in *The Fable of the Bees*:

> A man of honor must not cheat and tell a lie: he must punctually repay what he borrows at play, though the creditor has nothing to show for it, but he may drink and swear and owe money to all the tradesmen in town without taking notice of their dunning. A man of honour must be true to his prince and country, while he is in their service, but if he thinks himself not well used, he may quit it and do them all the mischief he can. A man of honour must never change his religion for interest, but he may be as debauched as he pleases and never practice any. He must make no attempts upon his friend's wife, daughter, sister or any-

body that is trusted to his care, but he may lie with all the world besides.[51]

In Montesquieu's characterization as well as in Mandeville's satire we can easily recognize traits which we have noticed before. These traits will be obstinately repeated by other authors. In Chapter VII of his *Deontology*, Jeremy Bentham, comparing the democratic and the aristocratic morality wrote: The first thinks that to pay one's debts in commercial relations is more important than to pay debts of honour, that to be injured is more important than to be ridiculed. The aristocratic morality is of a contrary opinion. The democratic opinion is for utilitarianism, i.e., thinks about the effects of our actions, while the aristocratic admits that taste has to decide about the choice of our action, and taste is purely personal.

The Gentleman

According to some writers, the prestige of England was enhanced to a higher degree by the export of the ideal of a gentleman than by the export of coal. E. Barker, however, in his book *Traditions of Civility*, treats this ideal as not specifically English but as an ideal born in Europe and derived from chivalry combined with the *cortegiano*.[52] It is an indisputable fact that the contribution of England in the creation of this concept was dominant. Many European countries accepted the word with the notion, thus filling a gap in their own vocabularies.

It is interesting to watch the successive definitions of the term "gentleman" in the different editions of the *Encyclopaedia Britannica*, or to go through the definitions given in the *Oxford English Dictionary* (1961 ed.). The first definition given in the dictionary stresses the importance of birth. A gentleman is a "man of gentle birth, or having the same heraldic status as those of gentle birth; properly one who is entitled to bear arms, though not ranking among the nobility, but also applied to a person of distinction without precise definition of rank." As early as Chaucer, at the end of the fourteenth century, more stress is laid upon qualities associated with birth. A gentleman is now defined as "a man in whom gentle birth is accompanied by appropriate qualities and behavior;

L

hence in general a man of chivalrous instincts and fine feelings."

Thomas Smith, in his *De republica anglorum* (1583) distinguishes four classes in English society: 1) gentleman, 2) citizens and burgesses, 3) yeomen, 4) artificers and laborers. Gentlemen were in turn divided into *nobilitas major* and *nobilitas minor*. The former was composed of knights with the title of "Sir." As to the latter we read: "Whoever studieth the laws of the realm, who studieth in the universities, who professeth liberal science, and, to be short, who can live idly without any manual labour and will bear the port, charge and countenance of a gentleman he . . . shall be called a gentleman." [53]

Against the argument that these conditions make the attainment of the status of a gentleman too easy, the author replies that a gentleman, as defined above, has many duties incumbent upon him. He must be more brave, more magnificent, he must keep about him idle servants, who shall do nothing, but wait upon him. He must array himself and arm in a way suitable to his rank. He must be more learned.

The discussion of who deserves the name of a gentleman which can be found at the beginning of the *Cortegiano* was still going on a century later. In 1662 Henry Peacham gives a detailed analysis of the problem in his book *The Complete Gentleman,* where the word "noble" is used interchangeably with the word "gentleman." [54] The first question to arise is whether persons of low birth can be admitted to the class of gentlemen. In order to support his pro attitude, the author recalls distinguished writers of antiquity who were of mean origin. Virgil was the son of a porter, Horace of a trumpeter, Theophrastus of a butcher. The second question he asks himself is whether a bastard may be said to be nobly born or not. The answer is positive because history shows that bastards were often more outstanding and meritorious than legal sons. Now the problem arises, can someone lose his nobility? If virtue can contribute to an advancement to nobility, it is clear that vice can deprive us of it, whereas poverty does not prevent us from being noble.

An interesting discussion follows about the status of different professions. The author is willing to include physicians among the nobles, with the reservation that his liberality does not concern "common chirurgeons, women doctors, mountebanks and unlettered empirics." The situation of merchants is more complicated. Peacham is prone to defend them against the unfavorable opinion of Aristotle. As no country is self-sufficient where goods are concerned, the merchants' work is of great utility. Although Peacham does not go so far as to admit them openly into the class of gentlemen, he includes the honest merchant among the benefactors of his country. Painters, stageplayers, fiddlers, jugglers, and so on cannot have any share in the nobility or gentry, as they labor for their livelihood and for gain. All mechanics and artists are in the same category.

As we can see from these remarks, Peacham does not attribute great importance to birth. His concept of nobility admits that its qualities can be lost and acquired, while nobility by birth is fixed forever. Middle class writers deny the importance of birth still more vigorously as they tend to adjust the model of a gentleman to their own aspirations. Daniel Defoe distinguishes between the gentleman by birth and the gentleman by breeding or by education. We shall return to him later on.

Let us extract from our considerations a picture of the complete gentleman. As early as the fourteenth century, noble birth was not thought a sufficient condition for being a gentleman. By the time of Thomas Smith, in the sixteenth century, it was no longer a necessary condition. What was obstinately repeated throughout the centuries was the impossibility of being a gentleman if one was engaged in manual work. The famous saying,

> When Adam dug and Eve span
> Who was then the Gentleman?

implied that a gentleman was expected to be idle or at any rate not engaged in manual work. He could not accept any salaried employment and especially could not engage in trade. "There are many a younger brother of a great family," wrote Joseph Addison, "who had rather see their children starve like gentlemen than strive in a trade or profession that is beneath their quality. This humour fills several parts of Europe with pride and beggary." [55] "The word 'gentleman' in one of its vulgar acceptations," wrote John Stuart Mill, "meant any one who lived without labour, in another—without manual labour." [56] If a gentleman worked, his work had to be the work of an amateur, a disinterested hobby, an activity enjoyed for itself. It is interesting to note that many distinguished writers in England pretended that their manuscripts reached the publisher through the connivance of a friend who wanted to make them public. It was beneath the rank of a gentleman to give himself the trouble. Shaftesbury insisted that the publishing of his writings was his secretary's affair, to which he paid no attention. Work for a salary was repudiated because, among other reasons, it impeached a man's independence by submitting him to external control. One could not imagine Aristotle's *megalopsūchos* subservient to his employer.

The mental equipment expected of a gentleman was assessed differently by different authors. Peacham, who was a man of the Renaissance, stressed the importance of learning and of poetry and music. According to him, "poetry can turn brutishness into civility, make the lewd honest . . . turn hatred to love, cowardice into valor, and in brief, like a queen command over all affections." [57] Music also had beneficial effects. The bite of the tarantula could be cured only by music.

English writers agreed on the necessity of studying the law, as the gentleman was expected to take part in the ruling of his country and to be a governor.[58] "They hardly are to be admitted for noble, who, though of never so excellent parts, consume their light in a dark lanthorn in contemplation and a stoical retiredness." [59]

Latin and Greek were obligatory until the present day. It has been noticed many times that they played the role of a barrier, excluding from the rank of gentleman those who were not *taught* classical languages, although it was unimportant whether a gentleman had mastered them in fact or not.

It is a generally accepted opinion that the character of a gentleman was considered more important than his intellectual endowments. To be too intelligent, Aldous Huxley affirmed in one of his works, is to take the risk of not being a gentleman. A French ambassador in England warned foreigners intending to visit that country, not to be brilliant in society as this aroused suspicion rather than admiration. People from the continent were believed to assure their position in society by speaking, while an Englishman assured his position by keeping silent.

To distinguish himself from the vulgar was the constant concern of the gentleman, although, being rather a conformist, he had no ambition to distinguish himself from members of his own class. He assured his position by his manners: his speech, his way of eating and dressing, his courtesy. He was always very sensitive to the opinion he enjoyed among his equals.

The gentleman is cautious in his commitments but never fails to make good on what he has promised. Everybody knows the expression "gentleman's agreement," which means an agreement that is binding although not written. Being himself reliable, a gentleman trusted everybody and took everybody seriously. He respected the privacy of others.[60] He will not repeat what he has learned from someone, even though he is not explicitly asked to keep the information secret. He never takes advantage of the weakness of his adversaries.

As to his recreations, the gentleman has many available sports. Horseback riding and hunting are particularly suited to his rank. Travel has also to be included in his education. The knowledge derived from traveling was much appreciated by those who listened to Odysseus relate his adventures. It is a well-known fact that British aristocracy and upper-class had to go abroad to add a finishing touch to their education. Samuel Richardson, describing his hero Sir Charles Grandison in conformity with aristocratic patterns, did not forget to send him not only to the continent but also to the Middle East. In the twentieth century travel has ceased to be the privilege of the nobility and the wealthy.

Aesthetic elements in the picture of the gentleman must not be overlooked. He had to be the "ornament and delight of society." "All the great and solid perfections of life appear in the finished gentleman with a beautiful gloss and varnish; everything he says and does is accompanied with a manner or rather a charm, that draw the admiration and good will of every beholder." [61]

Taine was of the opinion that the idea of a gentleman was different from that of the French *gentilhomme*. "*Gentilhomme* awakens ideas of elegance, delicacy, tact, exquisite politeness, tender honour, cavalier turn, prodigal liberality, brilliant valour;

these were the salient traits of the superior class in France." A gentleman in England was characterized by "independent fortune, the style of the house, a certain exterior appearance, habits of luxury and ease. . . . Add to them for more cultivated minds a liberal education, travel, instruction, good manners, knowledge of the world." [62]

I do not think this comparison is very convincing because the differences proclaimed are not sufficiently demonstrated. Certainly different traits did exist, if only because of the difference in the political situation. After the French Revolution, the French nobility did not exercise any power, while the English patricians until the beginning of the twentieth century had a great share in the government of their country.

Before closing these remarks it is impossible to pass in silence Thorstein Veblen's book *The Theory of the Leisure Class.* Veblen did not make clear whether he was describing the American upper middle class or the aristocracy of any society perhaps even of a primitive society. Yet his book cannot be omitted from our considerations because it introduced concepts which have often proved useful in describing a way of life, such as the concepts of vicarious idleness, vicarious consumption, conspicuous consumption, and conspicuous waste. According to Veblen, in the leisure class nonindustrial occupations are as a rule more honorable. Among them, as I have already mentioned, government, warfare, religious observances, and sports are rated the highest. Whenever men in primitive society undertake an industrial occupation it must testify to an excellence which cannot be compared with the uneventful diligence of women. In primitive societies a leisure class usually emerges out of a predatory habit of life: warfare and hunting. When the survival of a society does not depend on warfare or hunting, then leisure is considered most appropriate to those who are at the top. When the master does not indulge in conspicuous leisure, he does so vicariously by having numerous unoccupied servants. To be surrounded by a number of subordinates gives him "a divine assurance" and "an imperious complaisance" of a man accustomed to rule. Servants are trained to support the honor of their master according to an elaborate ritual code.

The upper classes in Veblen's presentation indulge in conspicuous consumption, consuming only things rare and of exquisite taste. His household performs the function of vicarious consumers and waste constitutes one of the criteria of belonging to the privileged. In a small group a member of the upper class exhibits a waste of time. In large groups, where it is impossible to control the life of individuals, it proves more useful to resort to a conspicuous waste of goods. The ownership of things of no use enhances the prestige of their owner, for example, the ownership of meadows not exploited or of a large number of fast horses.

An unstained dress shows that one does not work in it. Dress must be costly and often changed. Women, by their idleness and by their dress, are called upon to demonstrate the life of leisure and consumption.

The upper class is conservative and conservatism serves as a mark of respectability. An inclination to provoke change is rather vulgar.

I fully agree with the critical remarks of C. Wright Mills made in the introduction to a recent edition of Veblen's book. Mills believes that Veblen underestimated the role of the elite and did not take into account that idleness could not be attributed to all its members. It could be, I think, attributed without restriction only to women, whose purely decorative functions in the upper middle class has been stressed by different authors.

In the successive definitions of a gentleman listed earlier one can watch the growing importance of what was called by Adkins cooperative values as opposed to competitive ones. Yet in Veblen's picture "invidious comparison" supports competitive excellences which are a survival of the predatory spirit.

In the ethos of the European nobility the notion of honor played a very important role as we well know. It would be interesting to examine in what kinds of groups this value can be expected to flourish. An emulative spirit is particularly evident among the Kwakiutl of Vancouver Island, with their craving for self-distinction and their conspicuous waste, known as potlatch. An attitude of dignity, a magnificence, the keeping of promises regardless of the cost was noticed among some pastoral mountain dwellers like those in the Tatras in Poland, before they became corrupted by tourists and yielded to the general uniformization of the country.

"Honor and shame," writes J. G. Peristiany, "are the constant preoccupation of individuals in small scale, exclusive societies, where face to face personal, as opposed to anonymous, relations are of paramount importance and where the social personality of the actor is as significant as his office." [63]

The observation that stress upon honor is typical of small groups with face to face relations is convincing and accounts for the chivalric spirit developed by the pastoral mountain dwellers mentioned above. However, this factor does not seem either necessary or sufficient to develop concern for honor. Honor, as I pointed out, may develop in stratified societies where a class, not necessarily characterized by face to face relations, has a feeling of superiority and tries to justify it and keep intruders at a safe distance. Pitt-Rivers admits that there is also a tendency to stress honor in groups living outside the law and points at certain similarities between street corner gangs and the aristocracy, both contemptuous of legality. Duelling among aristocrats was an example of an administration of justice which neglected state magistrates.[64] As a man of honor was characterized by pride and independence one could hardly expect the development of this kind of personality in groups which experienced long and humiliating oppression. The fact that the mountain dwellers of the Tatras have never been serfs contributed to their attitude.

I can only suggest questions here, without trying to answer them. It would be interesting to explain why the *Spartiatai* of ancient Sparta, although confined to military occupations, free from working for a livelihood, and united in their consciousness of superiority over the *helotes*, did not exhibit a sense of personal honor. Perhaps their gregariousness, described so vividly by Xenophon, did not promote competitive excellence.

The Bourgeois Morality

The ethos associated with chivalric traditions, which I tried to outline earlier, can be considered as an ideal type in Max Weber's sense. Treating it as a typological unit, we can look for this kind of way of life as we did in a previous section not only among the privileged in a stratified society but also outside this class. In doing so we make use of this concept in the same way that we make use of the concept of feudalism in ancient Greece or in Japan in the time of the samurai. Whenever we speak of feudalism we think of its classical form represented by medieval France. French feudalism is the typological unit to which we refer when considering feudalism in different epochs and different countries. Feudalism, in conditions different from those in medieval France, can approach this model more or less, without attaining it in all its historical details.

When we speak of puritan morality we can also treat it either as a historical phenomenon, represented by certain religious sects of Europe and America in a given period, or as a definite type of morality, characterized, for example, by a special attitude toward pleasure and sexual life. In this sense puritan morality has been attributed to the Soviet Union and to the Dobu tribe, as described by Ruth Benedict, in her book, *Patterns of Culture*.

It is less obvious that when we speak of Christian morality we have also a type of morality in mind. If we consider it as a historical phenomenon, we ought rather to speak of Christian moralities, as the teachings of St. Francis d'Assisi differ greatly from the Christian morality preached by Alfonso da Liguori. When Nietzsche in his *Genealogy of Morals* criticized Christian morality as the morality of the weak, who praised kindness and humanity in order to disable those who were strong, he had in mind again not a historical phenomenon but a *type* of morality in which soft, amiable virtues predominated.

In speaking of bourgeois morality I shall also try to reconstruct an ideal type. Its delineation, however, encounters a puzzling problem at the very start.

While it is not difficult to decide who belongs at the top of the ladder in a given society when noble birth is one of the criteria, the concept of middle class is very vague of course. In fact, different writers describing the middle class have had different groups in view. Thus, for example, W. Sombart, in his well-known book called *Der Bourgeois*, means by bourgeois an urban *homo economicus*, who takes part in the processes of production and distribution of goods in a capitalist system. This category is still more restricted by the fact that the author does not take into account the Jewish minority which he has described in a separate book.

When, in turn, E. Goblot, in his very interesting work called *La barrière et le niveau, Étude sociologique sur la bourgeoise française moderne* (Paris, 1925), characterizes his book as a study of the modern French bourgeoisie, he has in view a group constituted of people who belong to the so-called *société* but not to the aristocracy. In order to be admitted to this group, good manners, a certain income, and a higher education for men are required. This group is composed of professionals, like lawyers, physicians, and engineers, and constitutes a whole analogous to that called the "intelligentsia" in Eastern Europe.

While shopkeepers and artisans are not taken into account by Goblot, shopkeepers, artisans, and small whitecollar workers constitute the object of the Danish sociologist Svend Ranulf in his book, *Moral Indignation and Middle Class Psychology*, published in Copenhagen in 1938. This group is characterized first of all by the income of its members. Shopkeepers and artisans are also the people referred to by writers who attribute pacificism to the middle class. Professional soldiers who should also be included in it by reason of income or education are not taken into consideration.

Marxist literature in general and Marx and Engels themselves used the word "bourgeoisie" in a rather ambiguous way. Sometimes they meant all privileged persons as opposed to the proletariat. In this sense the gentry belonged to the bourgeoisie. At other times, the term referred to an urban class, at times in harmony with and at times opposed to the gentry. The lower middle class, according to the Marxist scheme, constituted the third class of the bourgeois society, who as everybody knows was composed of those who had the means of production but did not employ labor. This category included small artisans as well as small farmers, groups not usually included in the concept of petty bourgeoisie: the etymology of the word suggests its connection with urban life.

These examples show that one can easily be confused as to what groups are considered middle class. Two English writers, R. Lewis and A. Maude, deplore the vagueness of this concept in their book *The English Middle Class*, first published in 1949 (London). According to their jesting proposal, before the Second

World War one could include in the English middle class all
people who used napkin rings at their meals, in contradistinction
to the members of the upper class who changed their napkins at
every meal and to the proletariat who did not use them at all. But
this criterion ceased to be valid after the war, which brought many
changes in people's habits.

Whatever may be the criteria used to distinguish the middle
class, this class is by no means homogeneous. This fact is made
sufficiently clear by A. Meusel, author of the article entitled
"Middle-class" in the *Encyclopaedia of the Social Sciences*. Shopkeepers, artisans, white collar workers, teachers, and clergymen not
only have different traditions but different interests.

In order to avoid all difficulties connected with the concept of
middle class, I shall take as starting point a well-known fact,
namely, that in the second half of the nineteenth century one can
observe an attack upon the so-called bourgeois morality in several
countries of Europe. A picture of this morality may be drawn from
this criticism. One must, of course, remember that this picture is a
caricature, but we can visualize the type of morality we are looking
for on the basis of these materials.

The attack observed in nineteenth-century Europe was carried
on from three directions: from the leftists, from writers among the
gentry or writers sharing their ideals, and from the Bohemians who
very frequently allied themselves with the social left. In spite of
the far-reaching differences of these groups, their pictures of the
bourgeois morality were very much alike. This attack was very
strong in France, Germany, Norway, and Poland, although the
middle class played a different role in each of these countries. At
that time the word "bourgeois" acquired its pejorative sense. "I
call a bourgeois everyone whose thinking is mean," were the words
of the French novelist Gustave Flaubert.

Let us review the features most obstinately attributed to
bourgeois morality. I shall take into account the criticism of the
behavior of the bourgeois only so far as it was supposed to be
generally accepted by him and was in conformity with his ideals.

While upper class morality recommended that one distinguish oneself by outstanding deeds, the bourgeois was considered
as cherishing an ideal of mediocrity and avoiding any extremes not

in conformity with average behavior. The tendency to keep away from extremes was associated with fear of bold ideas. This attitude was thought to make the bourgeois peace-loving and reactionary. George Sorel in his book, *Matériaux d'une théorie du prolétariat* (Paris, 1929, first published in 1918) was of the opinion that this class gives the least trouble to rulers and constitutes the ideal of moralists, economists, and philanthropists. Whenever a bourgeois tried to have ideas of his own which could prove inconvenient for those in power, he could easily be tamed by an invitation to a party given by a member of the upper class, because, according to Sorel, he had a great respect for the social hierarchy. This trick, says Sorel, was frequently used by the French president Millerand. His bourgeois guest dropped his dangerous ideas at once, much honored by the invitation. He never failed to inform his concierge about this great honor as the concierge was a person who had a decisive voice in forming bourgeois public opinion in France.

While the upper class does not notice, or rather, pretends not to notice economic necessities, the bourgeois is absorbed by these problems. He thinks in terms of money and saves in order to secure a better lot to himself and his children. He neglects and disregards the present in order to assure security in the future. His attitude is that of renunciation and one of his most important slogans is, renounce in order to accumulate. Marx, in his well-known criticism contained in the *Saint Family*, believed that the bourgeois in order to live missed what made life worth living.

The bourgeois morality has often been characterized as that of rigorism. Svend Ranulf, in the book cited above, tries to prove that, whenever the middle class comes into power, one can observe a growing severity in the penal law, a growing severity of blame in the press or in literature. This severity is the result of renunciation. Today we would use the word "frustration." The author, in his earlier book, *Jealousy of the Gods and Criminal Law in Athens, A Contribution to the Sociology of Moral Indignation* [65] endeavors to show that moral indignation—that is, a disinterested inclination to inflict punishment—is in fact a disguised envy. The desire to inflict punishment is, in his opinion, disinterested when it comes from a person who is not an affected party. According to Ranulf, we do not find this inclination in, for example, the heroes of the

Iliad. Whenever a man or a god in Homer's poems inflicts punishment it is because he has been *personally* offended. In the fifth century B.C., gods as well as men began to insist on severe punishment *where their interests were not involved*. Ranulf attributes this change to the growing influence of the middle class. The upper classes, with their feeling of superiority, did not exhibit a tendency to rigorism. The concepts of guilt, of sin, of punishments in hell never played an important role in this class. Both Sombart and Ranulf agree that envy constitutes a motivating power in the bourgeois ethos. But while Ranulf sees envy as the result of an imposed discipline of renunciation, Sombart sees in it the cause of emphasizing vitures like thrift and diligence which were obviously opposed to those of which the upper classes boasted.

The left wing attack against bourgeois morality stressed particularly the egoism of the middle class, its lack of civil virtues, its inability to cooperate, its confinement to immediate family interests. These were certainly features not peculiar to that class, but the bourgeois was in this attack a scapegoat who suffered for the guilt of others as well as his own.

While egoism combined with cheap sentimentality shocked Marx, the right wing as well as the Bohemians denounced the attitude of the bourgeois toward art and beauty. Aesthetic value judgments were closely associated with moral ones in upper class morality, but the bourgeois was considered absolutely insensitive to questions of beauty. His attitude toward art was proverbial. When painting was concerned he was expected to appreciate only a good imitation of reality. From de Maupassant to Céline French literature abounded in satire on the bourgeois spirit. It also found expression in the drawings of Daumier and Gavarni. In Germany the same antibourgeois spirit was expressed in music. Schumann's *Carnival* was written against the philistines. It ends in a march against the enemy. In England, Matthew Arnold (1822–1888) revolted against people absorbed by money-making and included them among the philistines. He said that they were stiff-necked, opposed to any novelty, and endowed with imperturbable common sense. Arnold pointed out philistines first of all among the middle class puritans. He wanted to free them from Hebrew traditions and guide them towards the Hellenic world.

By the twentieth century the so-called bourgeois morality had already assumed a definite shape, and the word "bourgeois" a pejorative meaning. It is interesting to note that even typically petty bourgeois movements like Fascism and Hitlerism used the word "bourgeois" with contempt. Both Mussolini and Goebbels did so. Hitler denounced bourgeois pacifism. Rudolf Hoess, chief of the Auschwitz concentration camp, tells in his autobiography of his education as a member of the SS troops. His colleagues were accused of having a bourgeois mentality if they refused to take part in acts of cruelty forced upon them as educational training. The German warrior was expected to be strong and never to yield to sentimental bourgeois scruples.

In his book *Escape from Freedom*, Erich Fromm attributed to the middle class throughout history a love of the strong, hatred of the weak, pettiness, hostility, thriftiness with feelings as well as with money, and asceticism. The outlook of the bourgeois was narrow, "they suspected and hated the stranger, and they were curious and envious of their acquaintances, rationalizing their envy as moral indignation. Their whole life was based on the principle of scarcity—economically as well as psychologically." [66]

As we see, the petty bourgeois, who in Germany had to pay with his laboriously accumulated savings the cost of the First World War, was not appreciated. In Marxist literature the word "bourgeois" was so frequently used to denote something hateful and repulsive that it gradually lost any definite descriptive sense and functioned only as a manifestation of disapproval.

Benjamin Franklin

Having drawn a caricature of the bourgeois ethos, I should like to discover the original who sat for the painters. In other words, I should like to look for authors who propagated *as positive* the slogans and values that were depreciated by their critics.

It seems advisable first of all to give attention to that epoch in which the middle class was gradually coming into power. Beginning in seventeenth-century Europe, a number of bourgeois writers emphasized the importance of middle class professions and contrasted their ideals with those of the nobility. Let us take as an example James Savary's book, *Le parfait négociant* (*The Perfect Trader*). It was written in 1675 at the request of Colbert, the minister of Louis XIII.

The book contains a eulogy of trade, especially wholesale trade. In the author's opinion, trade was created by God in order to foster harmony and love among people. God purposely distributed goods unequally in order to make people dependent on each other. The wealth of the country depends on trade. Trade pays the cost of wars, supports the court, gives to life all its charms. Eulogies of this kind were later repeated almost word for word by a number of bourgeois writers like Daniel Defoe and Richard Steele. They were usually followed by an enumeration of the virtues which the trader had to possess.

In order to make a list of bourgeois virtues, we shall take as representative of the bourgeois ideology, Benjamin Franklin in America, Daniel Defoe in England, and C. F. Volney in France. Franklin and Defoe were contemporaries. Volney was active after the French middle class came to power, occupying a position analogous to that of Defoe, although the latter preceded him by half a century.

Since the time of Max Weber, Franklin has been consistently mentioned in connection with the development of a bourgeois morality and was called the first bourgeois by one of his biographers. Historians of ethics do not usually mention his name because they are concerned only with the moral teachings of academic philosophers. But whoever tries to reconstruct the moral life of people cannot pass by this influential person. Both he and his teachings were very popular in France and his *Poor Richard's Almanack* wandered all the way to Poland.

The attitude recommended by Franklin is directed toward a worldly success. In order to be successful one has to rely upon oneself and not upon any supernatural power. Virtue is to be measured by its utility. In a famous lecture given to the lodge of the Masons in 1735, under the title "Self denial not the essence of virtue," Franklin opposes the opinion that virtuous actions must be measured by the effort needed for their accomplishment. He treats as lunatic anyone who gives preference to a course of action simply because it is against his inclinations. Duty is not beneficial because it is commanded but it is commanded because it is beneficial. Thus it is in our interest to be virtuous and no qualities are so likely to make a poor man's fortune as those of probity and integrity.

Religion was also looked upon by Franklin from the point of view of its utility. It was beneficial to a man to believe in the immortality of the soul, in a God who protected people and rewarded or punished them after death.

Franklin was considered by Max Weber to be the apostle of the ideal of a man worthy of credit. A man worthy of credit has not only to be industrious and frugal but he must appear as such. Thus he has to dress plainly, avoid being seen in taverns, and be always at work. "The sound of your hammer at five in the morning, or nine at night, heard by your creditor, makes him easy six months longer." Instead of the conspicuous leisure of the upper classes, we have here to do with conspicuous industry. "A sleeping fox catches no poultry," recommended Poor Richard.

In order to gain the reputation of a man worthy of credit, one must be punctual in one's dealings and conspicuously avoid waste. Not only one's budget but one's whole life must be planned in a methodical way. We know from Franklin's autobiography how he was methodically progressing in thirteen virtues which he considered particularly important. These were: temperance, silence, order, resolution, frugality, industry, sincerity, justice, moderation, cleanliness, tranquillity, chastity, humility. As to the last two virtues, according to his own words, he did not arrive at complete success.

Franklin connected order with foresight and foresight with caution and prudence. "Love your neighbor; yet do not pull down your hedge." "There is none deceived but he that trusts." But what was central to Franklin's teachings was, according to most of his interpreters, his attitude toward money. He was the first author to voice the new capitalist attitude, in contrast to the attitude which Weber calls traditional, that is, the attitude of people who, when better paid for their work, reduced the number of working hours, preferring more leisure to more money.

Franklin's views were recommended in the United States

until the beginning of our century. Horatio Alger was a well-known writer of rags-to-riches stories and when he died in 1899 he had many imitators.

Two centuries after Franklin's *Almanack*, Robert S. Lynd and Helen Merrill Lynd published their classic study of an inland city in the United States, called by the fictitious name of Middletown. Middletown was a town of small businesses, especially well chosen for a study of lower middle class attitudes. Investigations lasting from 1920 to 1929 led to the publication in 1929 of a book called *Middletown*. The further development of the town was watched until 1935, and in 1937 a second volume was published under the title *Middletown in Transition*. The catechism of an average resident of the town extracted by the authors from their materials and given on pages 403–418 may serve as an example of the lasting influence of Franklin in his own country.

Daniel Defoe

No writer in the field of literature is so definitely the mouth-piece of the commercial middle class of his day—thus one of the French historians wrote about Defoe. This opinion is widely shared and seems justified. It accounts for my choice.

Defoe's picture of the ideal personality is to be found in *The Complete English Tradesman, The Complete English Gentleman*, and *Robinson Crusoe*. We know from Franklin's autobiography that he was impressed by Defoe's opinions.

According to Defoe, tradesmen are a public blessing. England must be proud first of all because of her mercantile pursuits. Trade accounts for the power of England more than do her military achievements. King Charles II was justified when he used to repeat that English tradesmen constitute her real nobility. Defoe is quite aware of the importance of money, "the grand essential," as he calls it. In *The Complete English Gentleman* (written in 1728–1729 and published after Defoe's death), a tradesman accused by a squire of not being a gentleman replies, "But I can buy a gentleman." Like Franklin, Defoe considers money an important condition of being virtuous. "Where vice prevails, the great temp-

M

tation is want of money more than inclination," he says in *The True-Born Englishman*.

Robinson Crusoe is the embodiment of values represented by the bourgeois ideal of a self-made man. As we remember, the main incentive of Robinson to leave his home and sail far away is his determination to be rich. The book cannot be treated as a eulogy of primitive life, although Rousseau recommended it for that reason. After the hero's shipwreck he saves all the remnants of civilization he can in order to achieve maximum comfort.[67] In order to survive he must adopt all the so-called bourgeois virtues: foresight, frugality, thrift, patience, order, caution. His respect for bookkeeping is manifested in his inventories of the things he possesses, the things he has brought from the ship, natives he kills, positive and negative sides of his present condition. He is shipwrecked on a deserted island—this is a loss. But he is alive, while his companions were drowned—this is a gain. He is deprived of his clothes; but he happens to land on a warm island where clothing is not much needed—a gain. A tradesman's books, like a Christian's conscience should always be kept clean and neat. This was Defoe's motto, which he rarely followed in his private life.

Many critics of Robinson Crusoe have stressed his poor emotional equipment. He has no attachment to his devoted slave Xury, whom he sells without hesitation, and no regard for the beauty of nature. Only once does he note the quiet surface of the sea and this is when he is suffering from seasickness. When he meets a compatriot after twenty-nine years, emotion does not prevent him from thinking first of his monetary interests. He promises to help the captain in exchange for free passage to London for himself and his servant. As Robinson has succeeded in saving a quite substantial sum of money from the ship, this bargaining is not a matter of necessity. It is a well-internalized attitude.[68]

In *The Complete English Gentleman*, Defoe distinguishes two categories of gentlemen, gentlemen by birth and gentlemen by education or upbringing. He fiercely attacks the first and exhibits an ardent desire to belong to the second. The eldest sons of the gentry are uneducated. Their tutors never require any exertion from them because they are afraid of losing their job. The conversation of the future heir is confined to hunting and dogs. He is unable to write a letter without mistakes. He is aggressive, noisy, and vulgar. His estate does not interest him and he treats the waste of money as his calling.

The proper gentleman is the gentleman by upbringing. Having knocked down the barrier of birth, Defoe attacks the barrier constituted by liberal education and the knowledge of Greek and Latin. Why should we not teach students in their own language? Why should we not acquaint them with the Ancients in English? "A gentleman may be a scholar without Greek or Latin." And he may be a scholar although he has not attended any university and has cultivated his knowledge only by reading. Very often, Defoe concedes, it is not possible to treat as gentlemen the first generation of traders. But the door to the upper class must be open for the politer son. "The next age quite alters the case." His origin may be as modest and insignificant as possible, but if he has been to school, has completed his education by travel, reading, and conversation, and above all has a modest, courteous, gentlemanlike behavior, you can despise him as you wish, yet he will be a gentleman, not for his birth but for his personal merits. Manners could be acquired and thus they were stressed not only by those who defended their social status against an invasion from below but also by those who desired to raise themselves or at least their children to a better position on the social ladder.

The ideal personalities described by Franklin and Defoe have many traits in common: self-reliance, thrift, frugality. Both authors have a respect for science, a respect particularly noticeable in Franklin, who very successfully participated in the advancement of learning, neither of them liked the clergy and, when their religious faith was concerned, both were rather close to the deists. I stress this last point against Weber's opinion that early bourgeois thought was associated with puritanism. Franklin was a man of the Enlightenment and not a puritan.

In spite of certain analogies, the general climate of Franklin's teachings is very different from that of Defoe's works. Defoe was absorbed by his aspirations. His perfect gentleman had to be temporarily endowed with bourgeois virtues because they were necessary to make money. Once successful, he was expected to buy an estate and imitate the gentry. This idea was foreign to Franklin, who was satisfied by the accumulation of wealth and enjoyed the human respect due him as a self-made man.

C. F. Volney

Constantin François Chassebeuf Volney is very little known. He lived during the French Revolution. The National Assembly was in need of a moral code which could be used for teaching a secular morality, based not on religion but on "natural sentiment and reason." Volney's code, which was expected to satisfy this need, appeared in 1793 and has often been treated as a commentary to the Declaration of Rights. It bore the title *Natural Law or the Catechism of the French Citizen* (*La loi naturelle ou catéchisme du citoyen français*). According to the author, his code was as rigorously demonstrated as the statements of physics or mathematics since it was based on the biological constitution of man. The code was obviously meant to oppose the Decalogue. It was formulated in ten short questions and answers, to show the analogy as well as the fundamental differences. The law of nature which was expected to constitute its basis was formulated as the postulate, "Preserve yourself" ("Conserve-toi"). This postulate was thought to be derived from the fundamental fact that all people wish to survive, to avoid pain and be happy, and that all people justifiably think first of themselves.

Let us see how Volney imagined a man who would follow the commandments of his catechism. His virtue would not consist in renunciation (a common opinion of the time shared by Franklin, Hume, and Helvetius, and typical of writers opposing religious ethics). He was allowed to seek his own good and had to promote the interests of others only so far as this entitled him to reciprocity. In order to preserve himself he had to be enlightened, to have command over his passions, to be brave and active. Idleness was the mother of all vices. "To work is to pray" ("Travailler, c'est prier"). Poverty was not in the least a virtue. Volney agreed with Franklin that it is hard for an empty sack to stand upright. In his teaching the word "*honnête*" changed its meaning, when compared to the use of the word "*honnête*" by Chevalier de Méré. To

Volney it meant financial reliability. Volney's *honnête homme* had to produce more than he consumed, and a well-balanced budget was the criterion of his virtue. "The virtues of man and his vices can be in an infallible way appreciated on the basis of the proportion of man's expenditure and his income." Reliability in keeping financial obligations was a proof of righteousness. In general, the attitude of a man toward money was symptomatic of his moral worth.

By nature man had no obligations to others and in relation to his neighbors he had to keep a balance between give and take (*la balance du donné au rendu*). Because of the reciprocity expected for services, virtue was useful to everybody. No disinterestedness was expected to those who practiced it. Every crime was just as Bentham thought the result of wrong calculation and virtue was always rewarding. The fact that renunciation was not needed guaranteed that moral rules would not be transgressed.

There is a popular opinion that social classes in their ascendance to power preach asceticism and renunciation and that after their victory they indulge in a hedonist ethic. In order to illustrate this theory one refers usually to the time of Oliver Cromwell, as compared with the Restoration, or to the rigorism preached by the Italian middle class before it came to power. French writers before the Revolution did not confirm this opinion. Helvetius and Holbach advocated hedonism and Volney's ethic suited the revolutionary as well as the postrevolutionary period. His code had several editions in the time of Guizot, the author of the famous slogan, *Enrichissez vous!*

Analogies between the teachings of Franklin and Volney are obvious. Both men criticize renunciation, cite utility as a criterion of virtue, praise industry, frugality, and prudence, are convinced that the proper attitude to money is essential to virtue. These similarities prove once more that the morality recommended by Franklin was not necessarily combined with Protestantism. Volney was a man brought up in Catholic traditions whose adherence to religion was limited to a vague belief in a Supreme Being.

Our data are now, I think, sufficient to show the difference between moral principles advocated by the nobility and by the middle class.

The nobility did not discuss money, since wealth was taken for granted. This does not mean, of course, that nobles were indifferent to gain, but a noble who was thinking in terms of gain had to conceal it instead of making it manifest. Frugality, if practiced, was hidden and magnificence was obligatory. The attitude of the nobility toward work was different from that of the middle class. Physical exertion was allowed by the nobility only in sports.

To distinguish oneself was, as we remember, the perpetual concern of the nobility. This involved distinction from the members of one's own class as well as distinction from the vulgar. The bourgeois ethos was not particularly interested in this point. Aesthetic considerations did not play any role in the bourgeois codes. Taste was no judge in matters of morals and grace was not obligatory in order to win the hearts of people.

Fusion of the Bourgeois Ethos and the Nobility Ethos

In the course of the nineteenth century, the middle class grew wealthy and became differentiated. Franklin's maxims no longer suited the upper middle class, which more and more imitated the way of life of the nobility, and were left for the lower middle class. The upper middle class achieved an interesting fusion of the noble and the middle class ethos, a fusion which would have been seen in changes in the concept of a gentleman. " 'Gentleman,' the odd, specifically English, hybrid of feudal lord and bourgeois," wrote Mary Beard in her *History of the Business Man*.[69]

Let me illustrate this fusion by referring to two outstanding novels, *The Forsyte Saga* by John Galsworthy and *Buddenbrooks* by Thomas Mann.

According to Galsworthy, during the sixty-four years of Queen Victoria's reign the upper middle class was formed, a class indistinguishable by its speech, outward appearance, morality, and habits from the nobility. In the preface he writes:

> If the upper middle class with other classes is destined to 'move on' into amorphism, here, pickled in these pages, it lies under glass for strollers in the wide and ill arranged museum of letters. Here it rests, preserved in its own juice: *The Sense of Prop-*

erty. . . . So many people have written and claimed that their families were the original of the Forsytes that one has been almost encouraged to believe in the typicality of an imagined species.

As we remember, the Hotch Potch club refused to admit Old Jolyon because he was "in trade." But young Jolyon was admitted, since he was educated at Eton and Cambridge. After retiring from land agency, a profession deplorable in his estimation, Swithin abandoned himself to "naturally aristocratic tastes, considering that a man of distinction should never have been allowed to soil his mind with work."

> It was Swithin who, following the impulse which sooner or later urges thereto some member of every great family, went to the Herald's Office, where they assured him that he was undoubtedly of the same family as the well-known Forsites with an 'i', whose coat of arms had in its upper part a pheasant. Swithin did not buy the coat of arms but after a time placed a pheasant upon his carriage, the buttons of his coachman and his writing paper. Imperceptibly the rest of his family absorbed the pheasant. Except Old Jolyon.

Imitating the aristocracy, Soames bought a rural estate and started a collection of pictures, as a picture gallery confirmed the aristocratic character of his possession. He was not a connoisseur and did not collect pictures to admire them. He treated them rather as a good investment. The disturbing element of beauty was to introduce itself into the family with Irene and young Jolyon.

Although imitating the way of life of the nobility, the upper middle class was bound to preserve some distinctive features connected with the instability of the position of its members. One of the nobility was not obliged to be on his guard in order to preserve his status, since it was fixed forever by birth. A poor aristocrat was still an aristocrat, while a bourgeois position was characterized by up and down mobility. Therefore the bourgeois had to cultivate visible marks of his status. The bourgeois of the upper middle class had not only to look distinguished but also to look respectable. Respectability was manifested in his dress as well as in the furniture of his study. One remembers the spotless suits of Soames. Some authors attribute to this desire to look respectable the change of fashion which was noticeable about 1835 in Europe. Eighteenth-century men wore bright colors, laces, jewels. Now they confined themselves to dark or neutral colors, wore stiff collars and plain shirts with starched fronts. Men no longer wore jewelry, except possibly a ring with a coat of arms. Jewels were left for women. Everything not very costly had to be abandoned, since it was easy to imitate.

A member of the upper middle class had to take care of his education. At least a short stay in the University was obligatory, not so much to learn something as to secure good connections and to polish one's manners, which needed a long and elaborate training. Sexual morality was much more rigorous in the upper middle class than in the nobility. Illegal unions, as I have already noted, were fully admitted among the aristocracy. "All were engaged in the same open conspiracy in which Society managed to depart from Victorian morality without deserting propriety." [70] "The overriding consideration was to prevent any exposure of misconduct to the lower classes. In that respect the code was rigid." [71] While members of the upper middle class were concerned with their distinction from the lower classes while trying to live in perfect conformity with the requirements of their own class, the aristocrats had no need to bother and could afford to be different within their own class. Barbara Tuchman treats the freedom to be different as a class characteristic of the Patricians. [72] They could afford to have their own way and to favor the exceptional. In fact, the number of eccentrics in the English aristrocracy was striking. Interesting examples can be found in Bertrand Russell's autobiography.

The distance between the middle class and the nobility was greater in France than in England. The nobility in England was in contact with the city because of the production of wool, while the French aristocracy was mainly concerned with agriculture, a concern which was accompanied by a conflict of interest with the urban population. [73] The interpenetration of bourgeois and noble traits was also promoted in England by primogeniture because younger sons often moved to town and engaged in business.

In 1925 a French writer, E. Goblot published a book which I have already cited, called *La barrière et le niveau*. This book illustrates a synthesis of the bourgeois and aristocratic patterns.

The "barrier" in the title means that the good society described by the author defended its territory against the infiltration of new-comers. The "level" stresses conformity required within the class. Heroic virtues were not admired because they were rare and as such rather embarrassing. The good society exhibited the traits of nobility such as a disdain for manual work and salaried profes-sional work, courtesy, delicacy of feeling, largesse, and at the same time respected financial obligations: "Generous like a gentleman and punctual like a tradesman." [74]

There is a well-known notion that a victorious class imposes upon the defeated class its hierarchy of values, its ideals of person-ality. The facts contradict this claim so far as France is concerned. Although the aristocarcy lost its political influence after the Revo-lution, it was still admired and imitated by the victorious middle class. One can watch this admiration in novels by Balzac and others up to the present day.

In *Buddenbrooks* by Thomas Mann we have to do with a family belonging to the patriciate of Lubeca, a town of old and venerable middle class traditions. The hero, Thomas Budden-brook, is a refined, elegant gentleman. His manners are as impecca-ble as his dress. These, as in the case of Soames Forsyte, give him a feeling of security. The town patriciate appreciates his grace and ease in business. A cult of dynasty is observed in the family. The most important events of familial life are recorded in a golden book and the heir inherits a ring which resembles those with coats of arms which the nobility wears. Tonia, Thomas' sister, under pressure of the family, gives up her love for a future physician. She knows what her relatives expect of her and will not distress them by a misalliance. Even as he imitates the aristocracy, Thomas Bud-denbrook at the same time feels superior to them because he manages his business affairs more efficiently. The landed aristocrat, von Maiboom, is financially unreliable and the only thing he is able to do, when his ruin is inevitable, is to commit suicide. Again, like the life of the Forsytes, the life of the Buddenbrooks is threatened by art and beauty. Thomas' wife has a life of her own, absorbed by music and a violinist whom she accompanies on the piano. Thomas' only son is much more interested in Bach than he is in his father's business.

The exclusiveness of the nobility in Germany lasted much longer than it did in England. But in the second half of the nineteenth century the owners of big industry added "von" to their names and supported costly castles built in the feudal style.[75]

In Chapter II, in closing my remarks concerning the role of economic factors in morality, I postponed discussion of the impact of social classes and their economic interests with the intention of returning to this subject after having distinguished two ideal types of morality in Chapter IV. The general results of my considerations on this subject may be summed up as follows.

The ideal type of the so-called bourgeois morality was extracted first of all from middle class writers, while the morality of the nobility was described on the basis of writings by aristocrats or writings which had them as objects. But there is no necessary connection between either of these types of morality and their respective class background. The bourgeois morality represented in our ideal type was, as we noticed, very similar to that professed by Hesiod in his *Works and Days*, although Hesiod had a quite different social position. The ethos of the nobility, in turn, could be observed, for example, in certain pastoral groups of mountain dwellers. The chivalric ideals appealed to middle class novelists like Samuel Richardson in England, and romanticism, represented mostly by middle class writers, was also under their spell. Utilitarianism in ethics, interpreted as a doctrine which judged actions according to their effects upon human happiness, was often considered a middle class doctrine. But the range of its supporters was very wide, from Thomas Chubb, a writer of low origin in England, to Baron Holbach in France. It must also be noted that if its supporters were recruited from bourgeois milieus, so also were its opponents, like Francis Hutcheson or Joseph Butler. Diderot, who was often said to represent with other encyclopedists the interests of the rising middle class, translated Shaftesbury, the aristocrat, obviously attracted by his opinions. It has often been argued that the call for tolerance, typical of the Enlightenment in general and the English Enlightenment in particular, was due to the middle class which wanted to do business with everybody regardless of differences of religious creed. But it was Shaftesbury, who had no interest in trade, who protested most vehemently against any interference with religious convictions. Thus, although I fully appreciate the role of economic class interests in the shaping of morality, I consider this factor as one among many others.

The Concept of Morality

As I come to the end of my considerations, I should like to return to the difficulties connected with the concept of morality which I raised at the beginning of this book. I pointed then to the fact that the situation of a sociology of morality is not essentially different from the situation of a sociology of religion or a sociology of art. Some people believe that religion must imply the existence of supernatural beings. Others argue that the distinction between sacred and profane is essential. Still others speak of religion whenever the concept of orthodoxy enters into account. This last, broad concept permits one to speak of religion even in the case of atheistic ideologies, if these are forced upon people under threat of treating them as heretics. Since the sociology of religion can boast of some achievements, it may also be possible to discuss questions of a sociology of morality without defining morality precisely. In fact, we were not under a necessity of having such a definition in the main part of our considerations, when we noticed that respect for human life may depend on the birth rate or that solidarity was enhanced by a division of labor. In all these cases it was sufficient to agree upon the moral character of the respect for human life or to count solidarity among moral values. Whenever the dependent variable proved to be of a nonmoral order we would only be guilty of trespassing.

Again, when theories concerning morality as a whole were concerned, the normal procedure was to test them by trying to falsify them. Here again it would be sufficient to point to a single phenomenon not fitting the theory and admitted to be moral, in order to prove that the theory in question did not work, at least with a universal quantifier.

The concept of morality shares the lot of concepts delineating a field of valuations. Morality is concerned with objects of praise or blame. A person who considers a type of behavior a matter of indifference will exclude it from the field of morality. Thus the scantiness of a bathing suit on a beach can make certain people indignant, while for others the matter is of an aesthetic and not a moral order. This fact makes it hopeless to find a definition which would satisfy the intuitions of all. People brought up in Christian traditions consider sexual morality especially important, while for others most of its problems deserve to be excluded from morality.

David Hume expressed the opinion that the distinction of moral virtues among other laudable endowments was not a fortunate legacy from the past. "The ancient moralists, the best models, made no material distinction among the different species of mental endowments and defects, but treated all alike under the appellation of virtues and vices, and made them indiscriminately the object of their moral reasonings." [76] Everybody knows that the word *arete* was attributed by the ancients to all laudable characteristics not only of men but also of animals. Prudence, which, according to Cicero, leads to the discovery of truth and preserves us from error and mistake, was cited by him in one breath with magnanimity and justice. In comparing great men of Greece and Rome, Plutarch enumerated, without making any distinction, all their blemishes and accomplishments of whatever kind. "His moral discourses contain the same free and natural censure of men and manners." [77]

This was, in Hume's opinion, the current practice of authors who did not associate morality with religion. The separation of moral virtues into their own field was due to the growing influence of religion. Philosophers, or rather divines under that disguise, seeing that some virtues and vices, because they are voluntary, can be rewarded or punished, singled them out into a separate class and called them moral.

Hume believed that this was unfortunate. What he called natural abilities, such as intellectual endowments or talents, were not different in any essential respect from the so-called moral virtues. He supported his theory by the following arguments.

1. Moral virtues do not enjoy such an important position as people usually think, a position which places them above all other values. Men are afraid of passing for good-natured as it can be taken for want of understanding and often boast of more debauches than they have really experienced in order to be taken for

men of spirit. It seems certain that self-satisfaction proceeds as much from courage as from mental excellences like ingenuity. People are deeply mortified whenever their memory presents them any past occurrence where they misbehaved with stupidity or ill manners. "And is not the chief object of vanity our bravery or learning, our wit or breeding, our eloquence or address, our taste or abilities? These we display with care, if not with ostentation; and we commonly show more ambition of excelling in them than even in the social virtues themselves. . . ." [78]

2. After showing that moral virtues do not deserve the exceptional position attributed to them, Hume contends that many of them are not voluntary. Courage, equanimity, patience, self-command, and so on depend very little or not at all on our choice. A passionate temper is censured more severely when expressed in a greater degree, yet it is then less voluntary.

3. Hume agrees that the approval bestowed upon natural abilities is somewhat different from that bestowed upon moral virtues, but sentiments raised by different moral virtues can also differ in quality from each other. Benevolence produces love, while justice produces esteem. Good sense and genius beget esteem, while wit and humor excite love. "Each of the virtues, even benevolence, justice, gratitude, integrity, excites a different sentiment or feeling in the spectator." [79]

4. The last argument supporting Hume's position is directed against the opinion that moral virtues are those which lead to action. Here also Hume does not see any reason to make a distinction between so-called natural abilities and moral virtues. Prudence, penetration, and sound judgment also lead to action.

These arguments explain why "all moralists whose judgment is not perverted by a strict adherence to a system" do not make any difference between laudable traits of character, listing benevolence in the same class as prudence, and penetration next to justice. All these virtues alike are useful to the person who possesses them as well as to others.

Let us begin with Hume's historical remark. It does not seem true that the ancients did not distinguish a separate category of moral approval and disapproval, and that the divines were the first to single it out. Socrates, in the dialogue, *Gorgias*, contended that it is better to be wronged than to wrong. What did he mean by "better"? "Better" to be sure did not mean here "more pleasant," as this would be a psychological statement obviously false. Aristotle in Book VII of his *Nichomachean Ethics* affirmed that he preferred a man who did something blamable urged by a strong passion, to a man who did the same without feeling any emotion. He considered it worse for a man to beat another without any feeling of anger than to do it in a fit of angry passion. This preference was again one of a moral order. In his *Topics* Aristotle treated as moral the question, whether it is better to be obedient to parents or to the law, when it is impossible to obey both. Examples of this kind could easily be multiplied and could be found not only in Aristotle but also in other philosophers of antiquity.

Thus Hume's historical remark is not convincing. As to the *meritum* of his contentions, it is easy to see that his inclination to obliterate the distinction between moral virtues and what he called natural abilities, like wit, good memory, or quick orientation, was due to the fact that he presupposed a general theory concerning value judgments. This theory proclaimed that whenever we approve of a type of behavior, we do so because of the pleasure derived from it. In the light of this theory and the fact that, by adopting it, we cannot draw any sharp line between the pleasure derived from a witty joke and the pleasure derived from someone's readiness to help, Hume concludes that there is no possibility (and no need) to distinguish moral virtues from other pleasant dispositions. His theory amounts to a refusal to distinguish moral values from other values on *psychological grounds*. But it leaves open the possibility of distinguishing them by criteria other than psychological.

Hume attributed to the clergy the separation of moral virtues from other virtues on the ground that the former were necessarily voluntary. Aristotle, as we remember, devoted the third book of his *Nichomachean Ethics* to the distinction between voluntary conduct and involuntary conduct, a distinction which he obviously treated as morally important.

I have cited Hume's opinion because it is the most radical one, going so far as to deny the rationality and usefulness of distinguishing a separate class of moral values. While I do not share his position, I am fully aware that any attempt at making this distinction clear encounters objections.

In the first part of this book I distinguished five groups of problems which could be found in books purporting to deal with ethics. These were: 1) problems concerned with the efficacity of our actions, which deserved to be treated separately and under the name of "praxiology;" 2) problems concerning the best way to attain happiness, which could be included in a "felicitology;" 3) problems related to values in general, which might be called general axiology; 4) problems of how to organize interhuman relations in order to achieve harmony; and 5) problems concerning the ideal of personality which one would like to see realized by people linked by these harmonious relations. As I favor the emancipation of the first three of these groups I set them aside. Let us look now more closely at the remaining two.

The first difficulty which I should like to point out is the position of the so-called prudential ethic. Joseph Butler, an English philosopher of the eighteenth century, considered that virtues like prudence, temperance, and thrift, being useful to the persons who possessed them, did not belong in the category of moral virtues. The moralist, according to him, was not interested in conduct beneficial or detrimental to the agent. He intervened only when the interests of others were at stake. John Stuart Mill in his book, *On Liberty*, distinguished in a similar way between prudential and moral truths. We have no right, he contended, to interfere with a person's abuse of alcohol if his conduct is detrimental only to himself, because his abuse is a breach of a prudential but not a moral truth.

The personal utility of such virtues as perseverance, self-control, industry, punctuality, and accuracy is obvious. They are helpful for the realization of our personal goals, no matter what these goals are or whether they are approved or disapproved. They serve the interests of those who wish to become rich, who want to master a new skill or a new profession, as well as those who are preparing to rob a bank. If we were to exclude these virtues from the category of moral virtues, the morality of the middle class would be reduced to almost nothing because as we have seen it was composed primarily of prudential virtues as exemplified in Franklin's *Almanack* or in *Robinson Crusoe*.

The uncertainty as to the proper place of prudential ethic constitutes the first, very important and controversial question which has to be answered in order to define morality. And in case of a decision to eliminate prudential truths from moral commandments one must face the difficulty of drawing a line dividing them.

The second point which I should like to make is connected with the intervention of the ideal of personality in our moral approval and disapproval. I mentioned above moral commandments whose role consisted in making interhuman relations smooth. But this role happens to be in disagreement with certain ideals of personality. In order to avoid conflicts it would certainly be advisable to have a society composed of conformists, a society of docile sheep deprived of any independent thought. We protest against such a society in the name of the ideal of personality, in the name of human dignity. Whenever the concept of dignity is involved in our considerations, the characteristic of moral norms as norms which are intended to eliminate friction proves unsatisfactory. The same holds true of the opinion that moral rules are expected to reduce unnecessary human suffering and to promote general happiness. An employee who flatters his superior in order to obtain some favor is not worthy of approval, although his adulation pleases his superior and although he himself can take a pleasant profit out of his behavior. The fact that the flatterer degrades himself is relevant here and provokes our disapproval. It is a new element which has to be taken into account. We think of human dignity when we disapprove of some forms of coercion, when we disapprove of capital punishment, of slavery, of parents forcing their daughter into marriage. In his *Treatise on Government* Locke considered as fundamental the rule that no man can exercise empire over another, unless he is authorized by him to do so. It is not human suffering which is taken into account here, just as human suffering is not what we consider when we speak of human rights. An adult has the right to dispose of his own person, has the right to true information from his government, has the right to free expression, not because he would suffer if deprived of it, but because it is degrading to refuse him the fulfillment of conditions necessary to the development of his personality. Conditioning children in a given way has as a result that, when grown up, they will *want* to do what they *have* to do. Although no suffering is involved, we revolt against the picture of such an education described by Aldous Huxley in *Brave New World*. The notion of dignity permeates our moral rules. When we speak of the happiness which morality is to assure, we do not think of the happiness of a drunkard who spends his life in alternate drinking and sleeping, but of a happiness worthy of man, that is, the happiness of a man as he ought to be. An ideal of personality is here tacitly assumed, and we must refer to it whenever we speak of dignity, honor, degradation, and so on.

The presence of this trend of thought in our morality complicates the picture drawn by utilitarians, who overlooked its existence. It also complicates a definition of morality which would take into account the *content* of moral rules. However, it does leave open the possibility of referring to some purely formal characteristics. Of these, three I think deserve particular attention.

1. Some authors, and among them Nicolai Hartmann, consider as a special feature of moral values the fact that they are built upon values of nonmoral order, that they need the existence of the latter. Killing is wrong because life is precious, theft is wrong because the objects we own represent a value for us, slander is prohibited because we attribute a great importance to the opinion we enjoy, to cause unnecessary suffering is wrong because suffering is an evil generally avoided. This dependence of moral values on nonmoral ones can be interpreted in two ways: as the *logical* necessity of building ethical systems on premises which are not moral, and as a *psychological* dependence between the fact that we consider pain undesirable and the fact that we prohibit it. This causal relation is exhibited in the case of a mother who scolds her child for maltreating a cat, saying, "Do not do that—it hurts."

While the dependence of moral values on nonmoral ones seems rightly observed in the case of moral commandments which concern interhuman relations, the situation is less clear in the case of moral values such as dignity. I suggest the problem without offering any ready solution.

2. A number of contemporary ethical writers consider univer-

N

sal applicability as a necessary condition to be fulfilled by a value judgment in order to be moral. Agreeing in words, they do not agree in their interpretation, which can assume four different aspects.

a) "It is only when a character is considered general, without reference to our particualr interest, that it causes such a feeling or sentiment as denominates it morally good or evil," wrote David Hume in his *Treatise of Human Nature*.[80] For Hume, when we utter a moral judgment we can take into account neither our immediate personal interests nor those of a particular person. In a given case we tend to solve a money conflict between a foolish rich old bachelor and a sensible poor father of a large family on behalf of the latter. But in order to appreciate it morally we must take into account the global results of accepting this solution in all similar cases; we must, in other words, consider it on a mass scale.[81]

b) Hume did not accept in moral valuations a regard either for one's own or for a particular person's interest. Some other writers require that a moral judgment disregard one's own interests and that one must be ready to approve or disapprove of the given conduct, no matter who is the agent. The indignation felt by somebody who learned that his house had been robbed in his absence would be moral, according to William McDougall, only so far as he was ready to experience the same reaction when learning about a similar event which did not concern himself. Only impartial approvals and disapprovals can be treated as moral.

c) According to the third interpretation, the readiness to extend our judgment from our particular situation to everyone who would act in a similar way in similar conditions, does not enter into account. What matters here is the necessity to formulate our value judgment so as to make it acceptable to the agent as well as to the person who was the object of his action. A moral judgment, according to Kurt Baier, serves to resolve conflicts, and as such, it cannot be biased. A moral point of view is the point of view of an independent, unbiassed, impartial, objective, dispassionate, disinterested observer.[82]

d) For the fourth and last interpretation, the possibility of generalizing a value judgment consists in the fact that any argument in its favor involves a reference to a general premise.

Ethical writers who referred to this criterion of morality used to cite Kant and his categorical imperative. In fact, Kant proposed to check a particular commandment by a mental experiment which consisted in imagining whether we should like to make it general. But while, according to Kant, this was to show whether the given rule *was right*, other writers wanted to show by this experiment whether the commandment *was moral*.

All these attempts at a definition of morality did not lead, of course, to a definition, but formulated necessary conditions which had to be fulfilled by a value judgment in order to make it moral. Whoever accepts this condition will be compelled to agree that moral judgments are extremely rare, since few people who formulate value judgments ask themselves whether they would be willing to generalize their opinion in any of the quoted interpretations. Thus moral valuations would be reduced to rare occasions in which we should probably hesitate over whether our criterion is the criterion of being a right judgment or of being a moral one.

3. I mentioned above two attempts at a formal characteristic of moral valuations. According to the third, moral valuations are distinguished from other valuations by an assymetry in dealing with oneself and with others. What I have in mind here is the fact that conduct concerning onself is valued differently from the same conduct directed toward others.

If in the distribution of goods I wrong myself, I am praised as a generous person. If I wrong others, I am disapproved. I am entitled to destroy my own property, but I cannot do the same with my neighbor's. I can risk my life, but I cannot endanger the life of someone else. If I wish to mortify my body as the ascetics did, I am allowed to do it. If I am obtrusive in defending somebody's rights I am not blamed, while I would be blamed for being importunate in defending myself. It is because of this asymmetry that we protest against Bentham's statement that our own pleasure and our own suffering has to be treated on equal terms with the pleasure and suffering of others. Bentham's disapproval of renouncing our own greater pleasure in order to assure a smaller pleasure to someone else would not be unanimously accepted.

Supposing that this assymetry is rightly observed, one is bound to ask whether it is a characteristic which can be attributed to all moral situations. The reply has to be, I think, negative. We can and even ought to defend our dignity, to resist pressure, when disobedience is necessary to keep our backbone intact. In the case of personal excellence we are entitled to think first of ourselves, because only personal merits give us the right to intervene in the way of life of another person.

The duality of civic and self-regarding virtues to which I pointed above makes difficult not only a definition of morality which would aspire to finding some common features in the *content* of moral judgments but also one which would confine itself to certain formal traits. The situation of the concept of morality reminds us of the situation of the concept of culture. If we were to include into the culture of a given society its language, its local religion, its ways of building habitations, its economics, its artistic achievements, it would be impossible to formulate any adequate theory concerning culture as a whole. Nevertheless, culture is the object of studies whose results cannot be contested.

Notes

Notes to Chapter I: Introductory Distinctions

1. Adam Smith, *The Theory of Moral Sentiments*, 5th ed. (London, 1781), Part I, sec. 1, ch. v.

2. Brand Blanshard, "Morality and Politics," in *Ethics and Society*, ed. by R. T. de George (New York, 1966), p. 2.

3. Robert Redfield, *The Primitive World and Its Transformations* (Ithaca, N.Y., 1953), p. 85.

4. *Ibid.*, p. 51.

5. Tadeusz Kotarbiński, *Praxiology: An Introduction to the Science of Efficient Action*, trans. from the Polish by O. Woytasiewicz (Oxford and Warsaw, 1965).

6. Stuart Carter Dodd, on clarifying human values: a step in the prediction of human valuing. *American Sociological Review* (1951), pp. 645–653.

7. Robert C. Angell, The moral integration of American Cities, *American Journal of Sociology*, vol. LVII (1951).

8. See Kenneth J. Arrow, *Social Choice and Individual Values* (New York, 1951).

9. Crane Brinton, *A History of Western Morals* (London, 1959), pp. 23–24.

10. Brussels, 1932.

11. *Fragen der Ethik* (Vienna, 1930). English trans. by David Rynin, *Problems of Ethics* (New York, 1962).

12. Voltaire. *A Philosophical Dictionary*, in *The Works of Voltaire*, vol. 10, trans. by William F. Flemings (New York, 1901), p. 164.

13. Bertrand Russell, *Human Society in Ethics and Politics* (Allen and Unwin, 1954), p. 28.

14. Emile Durkheim, *De la division du travail social* (Paris, 1893).

15. Charles L. Stevenson, *Ethics and language* (New Haven, 1944).

16. *The Nature of Moral Philosophy*, in G. E. Moore, *Philosophical Studies*, 2d ed. (London, 1948), p. 311.

17. See, for example, Edward Westermarck, *The Origin and Development of Moral Ideas* (London 1906, 1908).

Notes to Chapter II: Moral Phenomena as Dependent Variables

1. I quote from a French translation. *Les Prolegomènes d'Ibn Khaldoun* (Paris, 1934–1938), I, 177.

2. Gaston Bouthoul, *Traité de sociologie* (1946), p. 300.

3. Marcel Mauss, "Essai sur les variations saisonnières des sociétés Eskimos," *Année sociologique*, 1904–1905.

4. Ellsworth Huntington, *Mainsprings of Civilization* (Mentor Books, 1959).

5. *Ibid.*, p. 285.

6. *Ibid.*, pp. 291, 292.

7. *Ibid.*, p. 298, 299.

8. *The Works of Aristotle*, ed. by W. D. Ross (Oxford, 1924), Vol. XI, *Rhetorica*, Book 2.

9. Denys Clement Wyatt Harding, *Social Psychology and Individual Values* (London and New York, 1953).

10. Vilhelm Aubert, *The Hidden Society* (Totowa, N.J., 1965), p. 228.

11. This information is taken from Robert Redfield, *The Primitive World and Its Transformations* (Ithaca, N.Y., 1953), pp. 19–20. Redfield refers in it to P. Fejos' work on the Yagua.

12. David Riesman, *The Lonely Crowd* (New Haven, 1950).

13. I disagree completely with Lévy-Strauss when he considers potlatch as one of the forms of reciprocity. It is not an exchange of services but a competition for prestige by means of the destruction of wealth.

14. Huntington, *op. cit.*, pp. 162 ff.

15. *Ibid.*, p. 111.

16. J. M. Domenach, "Le modèle américain," *Esprit* (1960), Nos. 7–8.

17. Alexander Gerschenkron, "Reflections on Soviet Novels," *World Politics*, XII, No. 2 (Jan. 1960).

18. Alicja Iwańska, in *Bulletin 589*, Institute of Agricultural Sciences, State College of Washington, June, 1958, p. 12.

19. Khaldoun, *op. cit.*

20. Johan Huizinga, *Men and Ideas* (New York, 1959), p. 84.

21. Redfield, *op. cit.*, pp. ix, 22, 21.

22. "The position of someone who cannot read in a society where people can read is very different from being a member of a society in which no one can read." Margaret Mead, *Cultural Patterns and Technical Change* (Mentor Books, 1959), p. 14.

23. Redfield, *op. cit.*, pp. 57, 31.

24. See G. Freyer, "Morals and Social Change," *Proceedings of the Third International Congress of Sociology* (Amsterdam, 1956).

25. Khaldoun, *op. cit.*, I, 254.

26. Montesquieu, *The Spirit of the Laws*, I, 405, 342, 12.

27. Eugène Dupréel, *Traité de morale*, I, 249.

28. Oscar Lewis, *Five Families* (Basic Books, 1959), p. 2.

29. Oscar Lewis, *The Children of Sanchez* (Vintage Books, 1961), p. xxiv.

30. Ruth Benedict, *Patterns of Culture* (Mentor Books), pp. 155, 159.

31. Alfred Louis Kroeber, "The Morals of Uncivilized Peoples," *American Anthropologist*, XII (1910), 437–447.

32. J. Przyluski, "Introduction to an Anthology," *Religions of the East* (in Polish).

33. It would be interesting to study in detail the influence of private property, state property, and cooperative property (e.g., the kibbutz) on morality.

34. Montesquieu, *op. cit.*, Vol. II, Book 20.

35. D'Alembert. *Mélanges de littérature, d'histoire et de philosophie* (Amsterdam, 1767), vol. 2: *La morale des états*.

36. A similar attitude is to be found in the writings of Machiavelli and of the French diplomat Francois de Callières (1645–1717). See also *Le Secret des cours ou les mémoires de Walsingham, Secrétaire d'Etat sous la Reine Elisabeth, contenant les maximes de politiques necésaires aux courtisans et aux Ministres d'Etat* (Cologne, 1695).

37. This quotation is taken from the English summary of Stanisław Ossowski's work, *Selected Problems of Social Psychology* (in Polish), published in Vol. III of his collected works (Warsaw, 1967), p. 422.

38. Aristotle, *Politics*, Book V, 11.

39. W. H. Whyte, *The Organization Man* (New York, 1956), p. 7.

40. These are the results of empirical research done by M. Komarowsky and reproduced in her paper, "Functional Analysis of Sex Roles," *American Sociological Review*, XV, No. 4 (August, 1950).

41. I owe this tale to a Polish student of Gandhi's teachings and influence, Dr. Ija Pawłowska.

42. Margaret Mead, *Interpretive Statement* (New York, 1937), p. 488.

43. Benedict, *op. cit.*, p. 243.

44. *Ibid.*, p. 96.

45. M. and A. Edel, *Anthropology and Ethics* (Springfield, Ill., 1959), p. 74.

46. G. Glotz, *La Cité grecque* (Paris, 1928), p. 348.

47. Edward Christie Banfield, *The Moral Basis of a Backward Society* (Glencoe, Ill., 1959).

48. I quote from C. B. Watson, *Shakespeare and the Renaissance Concept of Honor* (Princeton, N.J., 1960), p. 140.

49. Richard Steele in No. 2 of the *Spectator* characterized Will Honeycomb as a man honest and respectable, when women were not concerned.

50. 1962, No. 1.

51. Richard T. la Piere, *The Freudian Ethic: An Analysis of the Subversion of the American Character* (New York, 1950), p. 53.

52. *Ibid.*, p. 64.

53. Thomas Burton Bottomore, *Sociology* (London, 1962), p. 232.

54. *Acta sociologica*, X, Fasc. 1–2.

55. Ethel M. Albert, "On Classification of Values," *American Anthropologist*, LVIII (April, 1958).

56. Polybius, Book IV, 20, 21.

57. David Bidney, *Theoretical Anthropology* (New York, 1953), ch. XIV.

58. L. T. Hobhouse, *Morals in Evolution: A Study in Comparative Ethics.* (London, 1906).

59. G. Lenski, *The Religious Factor: A Sociological Study of Religious Impact on Politics, Economics and Family Life* (New York, 1961), pp. 175, 176.

60. Maria Ossowska, "Moral and Legal Norms," *Journal of Philosophy*, LVII, No. 7 (March, 1960).

61. G. Ripert, *La règle morale et les obligations civiles*, 3d ed. (1935).

62. William Graham Sumner, *Folkways*, 1906.

63. By Puritanism Weber meant ascetic forms of Protestantism, like Calvinism, Methodism, and Pietism.

64. London, 1939.

65. Ruth Benedict, *The Chrysanthemum and the Sword* (Boston, 1946), pp. 222–223.

66. New York, 1937, p. 494.

67. G. Piers and M. Singer, *Shame and Guilt: A Psychoanalytic and Cultural Study* (Springfield, Ill., 1958).

68. *Ibid.*, p. 47.

69. Clyde Kluckhohn and Dorothea Leighton, *The Navaho* (Cambridge, Mass., 1946), pp. 106, 107, and 171.

70. H. Kelsen, *Vergeltung und Kausalität: Eine Soziologische Untersuchung* (The Hague, 1941).

71. E. Topitsch, *Vom Ursprung und Ende der Metaphysik* (Vienna, 1958).

72. I owe this quotation to Lewis Mumford's book *The Condition of Man* (New York, 1944), p. 334. Mumford called Engel's book "a sort of proletarian version of the *Fable of the Bees*."

73. Svend Ranulf, *Moral Indignation and Middle Class Psychology* (Copenhagen, 1938).

74. Alfred Charles Kinsey, *Sexual Behavior in the Human Female* (Philadelphia, 1953), p. viii.

75. In *The Ladies Home Journal*, Sept., 1964.

76. From the cited introduction to Kinsey's report.

77. *Op. cit.*

78. I am leaving aside the Negro problem in America.

79. March 12, 1712, Number 324.

Notes to Chapter III: Theories Concerning Morality as a Whole

1. Plato, *The Republic*, Book I, trans. by P. Shorey (London, 1946).

2. A. Kłoskowska, "Social Models and Mass Culture" (in Polish), *Przeglad Socjologiczny*, 1954.

3. "Chaque société a en gros la morale qu'il lui faut."

4. Clyde Kluckhohn, *Mirror for Man* (New York, 1959), p. 28. (First published in 1949).

5. Ward Hunt Goodenough, *Cooperation in Change: An Anthropological Approach to Community Development*, Science Editions (New York, 1966), pp. 72–74.

6. George Peter Murdock, *Social Structure* (New York, 1949), Chapter x, "Incest Taboos and their Extension."

7. This opinion may, however, be criticized in the light of the distinction between purpose and function made by Merton. Was it the purpose

of the incest taboo or its function to avoid conflicts within the family?

8. See Zoë Oldenbourg, *Le Bûcher de Montségur* (Paris, 1950), pp. 170–171.

9. I have in mind here not the magnates but the gentry of smaller calibre.

10. Robert King Merton, *Social Theory and Social Structure* (Glencoe, Ill., 1949).

11. Robert Redfield, *op. cit.*, p. 144.

12. See David Bidney, "The Concept of Value in Modern Anthropology," in *Anthropology Today*, ed. by A. L. Kroeber.

13. Redfield, *op. cit.*, p. 145.

14. Bertrand Russell, *Human Society in Ethics and Politics* (London, 1954), Part I, Ch. 1.

15. For a detailed analysis of both these concepts, see Arne Naess, *Objectivity of Norms: Two Directions of Precization* (Oslo, 1948; mimeographed), pp. 23–47.

16. See Naess, *op. cit.*

17. Dupréel, *op. cit.*, Vol. I.

18. *Ethics*, Vol. LXI, 1945, p. 41.

19. Charles Perelman, *De la justice* (Brussels, 1945).

20. *American Anthropologist*, XII (1910), 437–447.

21. *The Science of Man in the World Crisis*, ed. by Ralph Linton (New York, 1945).

22. L. L. Bernard, *Instinct: A Study in Social Psychology* (London and New York, 1924).

23. Alf Ross, "On the Logical Nature of Propositions of Value," *Theoria*, XI (1954).

24. C. I. Lewis, *An Analysis of Knowledge and Valuation* (La Salle, 1946), p. 414.

25. See C. Lévy-Strauss, *Tristes Tropiques* (Paris, 1945).

26. "Countermores are culture traits symbolized by the group as deviations from the mores, and yet are expected to occur." Bribery is cited here as an example as "it may be almost universally reprobated, yet it is taken for granted that some officials will succumb to temptation. A certain volume of countermores activities are thus 'normal' (in both a statistical and normative sense)." H. D. Lasswell and A. Kaplan, *Power and Society* (New Haven, 1950), pp. 49–50.

Notes to Chapter IV: The Nobility Ethos and the Bourgeois Ethos

1. A. W. H. Adkins, *Merit and Responsibility: A Study of Greek Values* (Oxford, 1960), p. 38.

2. O. R. Sandstrom, *A Study of Ethical Principles and Practices of Homeric Warfare* (Philadelphia, 1924), p. 67.

3. Quoted in Johan Huizinga, *Men and Ideas* (New York, 1959), p. 205.

4. Sandstrom, *op. cit.*

5. Adkins, *op. cit.*, p. 55.

6. M. Greaves, *The Blazon of Honour* (London, 1964), p. 104.

7. C. B. Watson, *Shakespeare and the Renaissance Concept of Honor* (Princeton, 1960), p. 151.

8. R. L. Kilgour, *The Decline of Chivalry* (Boston, 1937), Introduction.

9. *Ibid.*, p. 89. The French original is also given here, or may be found in Deschamps, *Oeuvres* (Paris, 1873–1903).

10. See Robert Graves, Introduction to Malory's *Le Morte Darthur* (A Mentor Classic, 1962).

11. N. L. Goodrich, *The Medieval Myths* (Mentor Books, 1961).

12. "Il est vain de faire une bonne action, si l'on ne veut pas qu'elle soit sue." Chrétien de Troyes, *Yvain ou le Chevalier au Lion* (Dell Publishing Company), p. 110.

13. Sidney Painter, *French Chivalry* (Ithaca, N.Y., 1957), p. 59.

14. *Ibid.*, pp. 31, 32.

15. Johan Huizinga, *The Waning of the Middle Ages* (New York, 1956), Ch. 7. First published in 1924.

16. Malory, *op. cit.*, p. 458.

17. *Ibid.*, p. 487.

18. *Ibid.*, p. 494.

19. I treated this subject at some length in a paper of which the summary was published in English in the *Transactions* of the III International Congress of Sociology (pp. 81–86) under the title "Changes in the Ethics of Fighting," pp. 81–86.

20. William G. Sumner and Albert G. Keller, *The Science of Society*, Vol. IV, "Rules of War."

22. Huizinga, *op. cit.*, Ch. 7.

22. F. J. C. Hearnshaw, "Chivalry," in *The Encyclopedia of the Social Sciences.*

23. Quoted in G. Cohen, *Histoire de la Chevalerie en France au Moyen Age* (Paris, 1949).

24. A. Hauser, *The Social History of Art* (1951) Vol. I, Ch. 8.

25. Greaves, *op. cit.*

26. The reader will find a discussion of the causes of the cult of women in the Middle Ages in Hauser, *op. cit.*

27. As to the historical explanations, it has been objected that Arabian poetry did not contain any adoration of women. I must add that the climate of Ovid's *Ars amandi* differs completely from that described in medieval legends.

28. The reader will find a detailed report of this criticism in Kilgour and Cohen, *op. cit.*

29. The practice of sending boys to boarding school in England has been treated as a heritage of the medieval usage of sending boys to court.

30. Malory, *op. cit.*, p. 452.

31. Kilgour, *op. cit.*, p. 13.

32. Stressed by both Kilgour and Huizinga.

33. Huizinga, *op. cit.*, Ch. 5.

34. I owe these details to Kilgour.

35. "We do not need these shopkeepers." Kilgour, *op. cit.*, p. 52.

36. Bertrand Russell, *Human Society in Ethics and Politics* (1954), pp. 42–43.

37. Huizinga, *op. cit.*, p. 59.

38. C. B. Watson, *op. cit.*, Ch. 2.

39. *De la vraie honnêteté*, III, 69–70, of the Works, ed. by Ass. of G. Budé (Paris, 1930). I translate *honnêteté* by "civility" as this translation seems the most adequate, the word having a different meaning from what it has today.

40. In the French court "il y a toujours eu de certains Faineans sans metier, mais qui n'étoient pas sans mérite, et qui ne songeoient qu'à bien vivre, et qu'à se produire de bon aire . . . ce sont d'ordinaire des Esprits doux et des coeurs tendres; des gens fiers et civils; hardis et modestes, qui ne sont ni avares ni ambitieux, qui ne s'empressent pas pour gouverner. . . . Ils n'ont guère pour but, que d'apporter la joie partout, et leur plus grand soin ne tend qu'à mériter de l'estime, et qu'à se faire aimer." *Ibid.*

41. Montesquieu, *The Spirit of the Laws*, Book III, Ch. 5.

42. The mental equipment prescribed by Chesterfield was mentioned when I discussed the qualities required of a politician.

43. 15 May 1749.

44. 10 January 1749.

45. Shaftesbury, *Soliloquy*, Part I, Sec. III, Par. 3.

46. Shaftesbury, *Miscellaneous Reflections*, Vol. III, p. 177, of "Characteristics."

47. 27 February 1749.

48. Montesquieu, *op. cit.*, Book I, Ch. 4.

49. *Ibid.*, Book III, Ch. 7.

50. *Ibid.*, Book IV, Ch. 2.

51. Mandeville, *Fable of the Bees*, Remark R.

52. E. Barker, *Traditions of Civility* (Cambridge, 1948), Ch. 5.

53. *Ibid.*, quoted, p. 130.

54. Henry Peacham, *The Complete Gentleman* (Ithaca, N.Y., 1962), Ch. 1.

55. *The Spectator*, 1711, No. 108.

56. John Stuart Mill, *System of Logic* (1875), II, 240.

57. Peacham, *op. cit.*, p. 92.

58. The word "governor" was used by Thomas Elyot in the title of his book *The Book of the Governor* (1531).

59. Peacham, *op. cit.*, p. 12.

60. According to E. A. Shils, this trait is absent in American culture, a culture which is populist or "wide open," developed without the influence of aristocratic patterns. See *The Torment of Secrecy* (London, 1956).

61. Richard Steele, in *The Guardian*, No. 34, 1713. Quoted in A. Smithe-Palmer, *The Ideal of a Gentleman, or a Mirror for Gentlefolks* (London), pp. 95–96.

62. Hippolite Taine, *Notes on England* (1874), pp. 173–176. Quoted in Smithe-Palmer, *op. cit.*, p. 48.

63. *Honour and Shame: The Values of Mediterranean Society*, ed. by J. G. Peristiany (London, 1965), Introduction.

64. *Ibid.*, Ch. 1, "Honour and Social Status," pp. 30–31.

65. Published in Danish in 1930 and in English first volume in 1933 and second volume in 1934.

66. Erich Fromm, *Escape from Freedom* (New York, 1941), p. 212.

67. A. A. Elistratowa, "Defoe," in *The History of English Literature*, in Russian (Moscow and Leningrad, 1945).

68. See P. Dottin, *Daniel Defoe et ses romans* (Paris, 1924).

69. Mary Beard, *History of the Business Man* (New York, 1938), p. 568.

70. Barbara Tuchman, *The Proud Tower* (Bantam Edition, 1967), p. 57.

71. *Ibid.*, p. 32.

72. *Ibid.*, pp. 4, 33.

73. Beard, *op. cit.*, p. 206.

74. This is a combination recommended by the *Spectator* and attributed to one of Sir Roger de Coverley's ancestors.

75. Beard, *op. cit.*, pp. 569 ff.

76. In his *Treatise*, in the Chapter "On Natural Abilities," and in the Appendix iv to the *Enquiry into the Principles of Morals* entitled "Of Some Verbal Disputes." *Hume's Moral and Political Philosophy*, ed. by H. D. Aiken (1948), p. 288.

77. *Ibid.*, p. 289.

78. *Ibid.*, p. 285.

79. David Hume, *Treatise of Natural Abilities* (Everyman's Library), II, 301.

80. David Hume, *Treatise of Human Nature, Ibid.*, p. 180.

81. *Ibid.*, p. 233.

82. Kurt Baier, *The Moral Point of View* (Ithaca, N.Y., 1958), p. 201. This criterion has lately been discussed also by R. Brandt, M. G. Singer, R. B. Hare, B. Mayo, and at some length by E. Hytten, *The Concept of Morality and the Criterions of Legitimate Argumentations* (Stockholm, 1959; mimeographed).